WILLIAM & HARRY

PREVIOUS: Nine-year-old Prince William and seven-year-old Prince Harry on the water ride at the British theme park Thorpe Park.

BELOW: The Princes sharing a joke with their father during a photo call held on the ski slopes in Klosters, Switzerland.

OPPOSITE: Princes William and Harry wait to greet guests at the service to celebrate the life of Diana, Princess of Wales outside the Guards Chapel in London in August 2007.

FOLLOWING PAGE: Princes William and Harry on stage, opening the Concert for Diana at Wembley Stadium in July 2007.

This edition published in 2008
For Reader's Digest Association (Canada) ULC
Canadian Contributing Editor: John David Gravenor
Manager, Book Editorial: Pamela Johnson
Vice President, Book Editorial: Robert Goyette

Copyright in text © 2008 Ingrid Seward
Copyright in design © 2008 Carlton Books Limited

Address any comments about *William & Harry* to:

The Reader's Digest Association (Canada) ULC
Book Editor
1100 René-Lévesque Blvd. West
Montreal, QC H3B 5H5

To order copies of *William & Harry*, call 1-800-465-0780

Visit our website at **rd.ca**

10 9 8 7 6 5 4 3 2 1

Project Editor: Gareth Jones
Copy Editor: Charlotte Judet
Designers: Katie Baxendale; Michelle Pickering
Picture Researcher: Stephen O'Kelly
Production: Sophie Martin

ISBN 978 0 88850 947 5

Printed and bound in Dubai

WILLIAM & HARRY

THE PEOPLE'S PRINCES

INGRID SEWARD

Reader's
Digest

❧ CONTENTS ❧

❧ INTRODUCTION ❧

It is over ten years since I sat with Diana, Princess of Wales, in her Kensington Palace sitting room, discussing Princes William and Harry, but I can remember it as clearly as if it were yesterday. It was a sultry morning in late June 1997 and I felt very scruffy as I perched on the yellow sofa sipping instant coffee with Diana beside me, the epitome of glamour despite the early hour. From her coiffed hair to her evenly tanned legs, she was pure Hollywood – an iconic figure but not in the least daunting, as when she spoke in her little girl voice she spoke as a friend and as one woman to another. Open and frank, her prime concern in her life at that juncture was "my boys," as she collectively called William and Harry. The year before – the year of her divorce – was, she confided, "the worst of my life." Now, however, she was confident again and brimming over with plans for her future and theirs.

Diana was conscious of the pitfalls that lay ahead for the monarchy as the Royal Family faced up to the difficult task of adapting itself to the demands of a world very different from the one even she was brought up in. But she was confident that the Princes would rise to this challenge – as indeed they have done, albeit in entirely different circumstances than she could ever have envisaged.

William, who was just 15 at the time, was still at Eton College while Harry, at 12, was in his last year at Ludgrove Prep School. Diana was surprised at how sophisticated her sons and all of their friends were, especially compared with her at a similar age, and she thought they were well equipped to deal with the problems of life. "William, being the intellectual one, finds it harder, but he is very aware of people and their feelings," she explained. "Harry is very artistic and sporty. He doesn't mind anything, which will help him too."

A couple of years earlier I had spoken to the Prince of Wales about these very same things. With far-sightedness, as it transpired, he told me that his main fears were what he would do if his children involved themselves in drugs and the ensuing publicity it would inevitably receive. He knew they moved in privileged circles where anything and everything is available – nearly all the public schools in the country have had drug problems at some time or another and often the

OPPOSITE: Princess Diana with Princes William and Harry, photographed by John Swannell in 1994.

7

better the school the worse the problem. His hope was that if he instilled good moral values in the boys they would be able to resist. As it turned out they didn't – or couldn't – and it was Harry who took the rap in a very public way.

Being who they are has given William and Harry a lot to contend with. Their childhood was a maelstrom of conflicting emotions that included argument, separation, divorce and death. This turned their lives upside-down and made them the stuff of an international soap opera. The stability so vital to children's development eluded them, and would produce problems, which even in adulthood they are still trying to resolve. Their unwelcome celebrity was one such issue. It would have been impossible not to feel important with so much attention directed at them and this, combined with the fact that no one ever said, "No," could so easily have given them the impression that they could get away with anything. The army put a stop to any chance of that happening, and both William and Harry have benefited enormously from the discipline and the camaraderie that comes with military life.

Through the force of their late mother's personality and beauty, the Royal Family of the '80s and '90s had become the subject of worldwide intrigue, the legacy of which fell upon William and Harry. Diana frequently complained about the media interest she aroused, yet was not averse to courting it when it suited her purposes. William saw first-hand the effect his mother's experiences had had on her, and he is honest enough to admit that his sometimes ambivalent attitude towards his position is a reaction to the stresses that Diana endured.

Although the Princes had hoped that the memorial concert and service for Diana in July 2007 would go some way toward allowing their mother to rest in peace, they must have known that this would never happen. The subsequent inquest into her death unleashed more conjecture, more personal details and more heartache for them, yet remarkably they have managed to make it through these tough times relatively unharmed. Inevitably they have both made mistakes, but have matured into well-balanced, responsible young men, who have benefited from their parents' diverse interests. Diana gave them a sense of their values as people rather than princes and developed their philanthropic consciousness; Prince Charles helped steer them gently towards maturity and refused to allow them to be stuffed into the straitjacket of royal tradition, as he was.

It is down to the Princes themselves, however, as to how they conduct their lives. They have amassed a group of loyal friends and allies, who are discreet

and trustworthy, thus allowing them to have something approaching a normal existence, although for them normal will always be a relative term. "Within our private lives and within certain other parts of our life we want to be as normal as possible," Harry said in 2007. "Yes it's hard, because in a certain respect we never will be, never can be."

Prince William is a future King of Great Britain and Harry is the next in line. The grandsons of Elizabeth II, they can trace their royal blood back over 1,000 years. Like it or not they are automatically separated from the rest of the world by their heritage. The guns that heralded their births have been replaced by photographer's lenses, through which the world has watched them grow from babes in their mother's arms, to proper British schoolboys, to grief-stricken young men walking behind their mother's coffin, to the adults we see now. We have observed every step of their subsequent progress and through the photographs in this book we will continue to do so with great affection.

ABOVE: Prince Charles with his sons, photographed by Mario Testino. The picture was taken to commemorate the twentieth birthday of Prince Harry.

CHAPTER ONE

❦ AN HEIR IS BORN ❦

At five o'clock on Monday 21 June 1982, 20-year-old Princess Diana, escorted by her husband The Prince of Wales, entered St. Mary's Hospital in Paddington, where Sir Alexander Fleming had discovered penicillin in 1928, by a side door. They took the lift to the fourth-floor Lindo wing, which is part of the historic hospital's maternity unit. Here the private patients give birth under the care of their gynecologists, one of whom was George Pinker, surgeon-gynecologist to the Royal Household and entrusted with looking after the Princess.

Diana had experienced a difficult pregnancy. Morning sickness and the daily media obsession with every detail of her life had stretched her mental and physical resources to their limit. So together with Prince Charles and George Pinker, Diana picked a suitable date to have the baby induced.

Everything was ready for the Princess. The adjacent rooms had been cleared of patients, a screen had been put up outside Diana's room, which was at the end of a corridor at the back of the hospital, and, as it was in the days before mobile phones, a private telephone line had been installed. But for a future queen the surroundings were not impressive. There was no ensuite bathroom and the furnishings were somewhat tatty.

None of this mattered to Diana, who was sick throughout the labour and ran a high temperature. Despite the epidural injection she had a difficult 11-hour labour, but was able to give birth without resorting to an emergency Caesarean section as had momentarily been feared.

At 9:03 p.m. on the evening of the summer solstice, Diana delivered a healthy 7-pound, 1½-ounce son. He had, according to his delighted father "a wisp of fair hair, sort of blondish, and blue eyes." Charles had been at Diana's side throughout the labour and left the hospital only when he was certain his wife and baby son were sleeping peacefully. As he left the hospital crowds sang, "For He's a Jolly Good Fellow" and called out to ask the baby's name. The Prince replied, "You'll have to ask my wife, we're having a bit of an argument about that."

From Kensington Palace he wrote to his friends, Hugh and Emilie van Cutsem: "I got back here just before midnight, utterly elated but quite shattered.

OPPOSITE: Princess Diana with her four-week-old son and heir to the throne, Prince William. This was his first official photograph and was taken by Lord Snowdon.

11

I can't tell you how excited and proud I am. He really does look surprisingly appetizing and has sausage fingers just like mine."

As befitting an heir presumptive, an official announcement was posted on the gates of Buckingham Palace and the Prime Minister, Margaret Thatcher, along with the heads of government of all Commonwealth countries were informed. The following day church bells were rung and a 41-gun salute was fired. Much to the delight of the crowds outside, the Queen came to the hospital to see her grandson and, according to Diana, dryly observed, "Thank goodness he hasn't got ears like his father."

Diana couldn't wait to get home, even if it meant running the gauntlet of the press waiting outside. After such a long labour Pinker knew what a big effort it would be for Diana to walk and move with ease, but he made a statement to the effect that he was perfectly happy with the arrangement, concealing any doubts he may have had. So less than 24 hours after arriving in the world "baby Wales," as he was known, was driven home to Kensington Palace to the secure arms of maternity nurse, Sister Ann Wallace, who was to help the Princess for the first few weeks. Diana needed help, as after the euphoria of the new baby and the excitement of showing him to everyone had worn off, she was left feeling deflated and exhausted as a result of post-natal depression, which manifested itself in tears and panic attacks. Even William's christening failed to raise her spirits and the only argument she won was the choice of the baby's name. "Nobody asked me when it [the christening] was suitable for William – 11 o'clock couldn't have been worse... I blubbed my eyes out. William started crying too. Well, he just sensed I wasn't exactly hunky-dory," she explained later.

The christening of Prince William Arthur Philip Louis of Wales took place in the Music Room at Buckingham Palace on the Queen Mother's eighty-second birthday, 4 August 1982, and Charles's wishes reigned. The only godparent near Diana's age was the Duchess of Westminster, known as "Tally." The other two female godparents were Princess Alexandra, a first cousin of the Queen, and Lady Susan Hussey, one of the Queen's senior ladies-in-waiting. Even more surprising was the choice of writer and explorer, Sir Laurens van der Post, who was 76 years old at the time. The decision to include van der Post was viewed with suspicion by some within the Church of England in the light of his advocacy of a generalized notion of faith rather than adherence to any one faith – a notion now espoused by the Prince of Wales. Prince Charles's explanation at the time was that he chose

ABOVE: Diana cuddles William during a photo call in Auckland, New Zealand in April 1983.

OPPOSITE: The Prince and Princess of Wales look on lovingly at baby William on the day of his christening at Buckingham Palace on 4 August 1982.

the mystic Sir Laurens because he was one of the best storytellers of all time. "I want my son to be able to sit at his godfather's knee and listen to his wonderful stories," he said. The other two godparents were the exiled King Constantine of Greece and Lord Romsey, Earl Mountbatten of Burma's grandson and a Gordonstoun School contemporary of Charles.

It was not an easy time as, just over two weeks before, horror had come to London. As a detachment of the Blues and Royals had trotted along South Carriage Road in Hyde Park, a car bomb exploded, killing two guardsmen and injuring 17 spectators. Seven army horses were either killed by the blast or had to be put down. Less than two hours later another bomb exploded under the bandstand in Regent's Park killing six soldiers and injuring dozens more. The outlawed Irish Republican Army admitted responsibility for the killings. Despite the Queen's anguish at the situation, the christening went ahead with the Archbishop of Canterbury, Robert Runcie, officiating. Afterwards a lunch party for 60 guests was held in Buckingham Palace's State Dining Room, with the christening cake, as is tradition, being the top layer of Charles and Diana's wedding cake.

Diana did not feel very well that day, which was made worse by the fact she felt excluded from proceedings, as endless pictures of the Queen, Queen Mother, Prince Charles and Prince William were taken. The decision not to include Diana in many of the photographs was deliberate on the part of the Palace, because in just six weeks the Princess had lost 40 pounds and looked ill and emaciated, as indeed she was. She managed to get through the lunch and then headed straight off for the relative sanctuary of Kensington Palace with baby William.

Diana may not have had her way about the christening arrangements, but she was determined her baby would be brought up in the way she wanted, not in what she perceived to be the stiff and starchy way Prince Charles was raised. Preoccupied by her public duties, Elizabeth, the young Queen, had been persuaded to place her son in the care of dependable, but prim and proper nannies, which was quite normal in the late 1940s when he was born. His parents therefore became shadowy and somewhat intimidating figures and it was the nannies that had day-to-day charge of his life and affections. Prince Philip, often away on his naval duties, missed Prince Charles's first three birthdays and yet was still somehow determined to mould his first-born son in his own image. It was an ambition doomed to failure, as they were completely different characters and have remained so to this day.

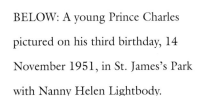

BELOW: A young Prince Charles pictured on his third birthday, 14 November 1951, in St. James's Park with Nanny Helen Lightbody.

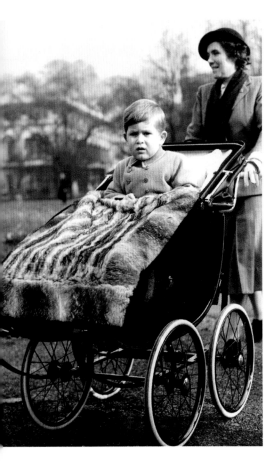

14

ABOVE: Prince William in February 1983, aged eight months, was able to push himself up unaided.

LEFT: Diana holds eight-month-old William up in her arms to make him laugh during a photo session at Kensington Palace.

FAR LEFT: Deputy Nanny, Olga Powell pushing William through the park in 1984.

LEFT: William arrives back from New Zealand in the arms of his nanny Barbara Barnes.

Diana was not having any of that and laid out her parental agenda soon after William's birth when she declared, "A child's stability arises mainly from the affection received from his parents and there is no substitute for affection." Nanny Barbara Barnes and her deputy, Olga Powell, were employed, but not as mother substitutes. "A mother's arms are so much more comforting," Diana explained, harking back to her own unhappy childhood experiences. Forty-two-year-old Barbara Barnes, with her friendly, no-nonsense approach seemed just what Diana was looking for. She was not formally trained but had accumulated her knowledge from experience and came highly recommended by her former employer, Lord Glenconner, a great friend of Princess Margaret. Sensible and practical, Barbara was careful not to interfere with Diana's upbringing of baby William; rather she guided her through the pitfalls and fears of looking after a newborn. Diana, at just 21 years old, and suffering from postnatal depression, was not easy to work for, but Nanny Barnes was sensitive enough to tread very carefully indeed.

Fortunately William was a healthy baby although he cried a great deal and made his presence felt from very early on. As Charles observed, "He gets noisier and angrier by the day," and even Diana admitted "he was a bit of a handful." Both parents were thrilled by their new arrival, who was pushed in his pram around Kensington Gardens by his nanny, just as his father had been before him. This time, however, despite the discreet presence of an armed bodyguard, rarely did anyone seeing the nanny and her tiny charge know who he was, possibly for the first and last time in his life.

In January 1983, Charles insisted that his wife get away from all the pressures at home and take a holiday. The choice of skiing at Liechtenstein's Prince Franz Joseph's Castle was not a great one. Hounded by press, Diana was constantly in tears and cut the holiday short, explaining to her hosts, "I cannot bear to be away from my son." It was a brief victory, as Diana knew. The royal couple were due to embark on a month-long tour of Australia and this time William would have to be left behind, which Diana dreaded. Relief came in an unexpected letter from the then Prime Minister of Australia, Malcolm Fraser, who wrote to Diana asking her if she would like to bring out William too. Charles was delighted as he knew the presence of their son would have a positive effect on Diana and present the young couple in a happy light to the Australian people, which would help to make the trip a success. "We can do six weeks instead of four and we can cover New Zealand as well so it would be perfect," he said. In taking William, Diana had broken with

OPPOSITE, BELOW: The Prince and Princess of Wales pose proudly with their son during their visit to Auckland, New Zealand, in April 1983.

another royal tradition: never before had a member of the Royal Family undertaken an overseas tour with such a young child. Contrary to opinion at the time, Diana never had an argument about it with the Queen – in fact she and Charles never consulted her – they just went ahead and included William.

On 22 March 1983 the royal party touched down in Alice Springs to be greeted by a small army of reporters and cameramen. Even after the 20-hour flight William, now nine months old, looked happy, if a little confused as he was carried down the aircraft steps. "Here's Billy the Kid!" one of the journalists shouted, causing Charles and Diana to smile. "From our standpoint they seemed like the perfect little family unit," another remarked later. Shortly after landing Barbara Barnes took William off on a private plane to a sheep station called Woomargama in the outback of New South Wales, which was to be the family base throughout their stay. "We were extremely happy there whenever we were allowed to escape," Charles wrote to friends. "The great joy was that we were totally alone together."

Spared the mass hysteria that greeted his parents wherever they went in the seclusion of his sheep station home, William developed quickly. On their rare visits Charles and Diana were delighted at his progress. "He looks horribly well and is expanding with visible and frightening rapidity." Charles dutifully wrote to his godmother, Lady Susan Hussey. "Today he actually crawled for the first time. We laughed and laughed with sheer hysterical pleasure." He later informed the van Cutsems how William was crawling at high speed and "knocking everything off tables and causing unbelievable destruction. He will be walking before long and it is the greatest possible fun."

It wasn't as easy for Diana as she missed William terribly when she was not with him, but at least he gave her something to talk about to the thousands of people she met. On a radio phone-in – something she had never done before – she was asked what William's favourite toy was. She answered with a giggle that it was a plastic whale that spouted water and which she put in the bath with him. It endeared her to the listeners and in the years to come she would rely on William updates to keep her audience amused and make them feel they knew her. She told of how he kept breaking his toys and once pressed the panic button in the Balmoral nursery, bringing policemen rushing to the scene. She also regaled them with stories of his pleasure at flushing anything he could lay his little hands on, including a pair of his father's shoes, down the toilet. She nicknamed him "Wombat," the "mini tornado."

OPPOSITE, ABOVE: Prince Charles holds William while his mother amuses him with a rattle at Kensington Palace in 1983.

OPPOSITE, BELOW: Prince William, aged 18 months, facing the cameras in his smart romper suit, in the walled garden of Kensington Palace.

By the time the royal party arrived in New Zealand, on the second leg of their tour, William was a source of fascination for everyone. The former nursery at Government House had been prepared for him and a grand old-fashioned pram, previously used by the Governor's children dusted off, so Nanny Barnes was able to take him for his daily walks around the grounds without being troubled by photographers desperate for a snap of the new royal celebrity. They got their chance soon enough as a photo call was arranged for William a few days later on the lawns of Government House. At nine o'clock in the morning television crews, photographers and reporters assembled near a large rug on the grass and waited for the "mini tornado" to make his appearance for his first photo call. They were not disappointed. Dressed in the height of traditional toddler elegance in a silk smocked romper suit, William crawled with great alacrity to the edge of the rug and lifted it up to see what was underneath. As soon as Diana replaced him in the centre of the rug he was off again, much to the amusement of the assembled company. "He performed like a true professional in front of the cameras," his proud father observed; sure enough William was getting used to being the centre of attention.

He toddled into the limelight again at the age of 18 months in the walled garden at Kensington Palace to speak that time-honoured word "Dada." Six months later he was back there again with an increased vocabulary. The media noted that he weighed 28 pounds, and was three feet tall. Diana noted that he loved the attention and was fascinated by the lens of a television camera.

The photographer John Scott remembered that Charles had been equally inquisitive at the same age. "He was precocious too," he said. "When he was three years old he could pronounce my Yugoslavian name, Colonel Vasa Vojinovic, as well as if he'd been brought up in Belgrade." Diana worried William was developing too fast, but circumstances were overtaking her and her inquisitive, self-possessed little boy. She was pregnant again and she hoped that the new arrival would teach him to share not only his possessions, but also his position at centre stage.

ABOVE, LEFT & RIGHT: In the walled garden of Kensington Palace Prince William stands on a bench between his parents. Later he grins at the cameras while his father strikes a serious pose.

OPPOSITE: A taste of life to come: William is fascinated by the television camera during the same photo call to celebrate his second birthday in 1984.

CHAPTER TWO

❧ ...AND A SPARE ❧

In January 1984 Diana discovered she was pregnant for the second time and everyone was delighted. Just before the announcement was made, Diana flew to Norway on her first official solo trip. She returned to a love note written by her husband, which read, "We were so proud of you," and was signed, "Willie Wombat and I."

Diana's second pregnancy was, however, no easier than her first. "I've not felt well since day one," she confessed. "I don't think I'm made for the production line." In spite of this, she kept up with her official engagements, the last of which was, fittingly enough, to open the Birthright Centre at King's College Hospital in London. She later recalled the time between the births of her two sons as a "total darkness" of which she couldn't remember much. But for the couple of months prior to the birth, she was very happy and recalled herself and Charles as being "very very close to each other."

Prince William was 20 months old and both parents felt he would be able to accept the new addition to the family without much difficulty. In fact Diana thought it would be a very good thing, as William was becoming thoroughly spoiled – not by his parents, but by the household at Highgrove and Kensington Palace. As one member of staff recalled, "He couldn't even fall down without at least a couple of people rushing to pick him up to see if he was all right."

As before, Prince Charles accompanied Diana to the Lindo Wing at St. Mary's Hospital, arriving at 7:30 a.m. on Saturday 15 September 1984 for the baby to be induced. At 4:20 p.m. that afternoon Diana gave birth to her second son. When Prince Charles emerged from the hospital a couple of hours later, he told the waiting crowd, "My wife is very well. The delivery couldn't have been better. It was much quicker this time." It was, however, a full nine hours and, he admitted, Diana was "very tired" and that he needed "a celebration drink."

According to Diana, she knew that Harry was going to be a boy as she had seen it on the scan. Charles was disappointed the baby was not a girl. His first comment was, "Oh God, it's a boy," and his second, "and he's even got red hair."

OPPOSITE: Newborn Prince Henry of Wales, known as Harry, in his mother's arms. This was his first official photograph after his birth on 15 September 1984, which was taken by Lord Snowdon.

If his father was slightly disappointed, Prince William was certainly not. He would have a little friend with whom he could play soccer, and he couldn't wait to see the new arrival. The following morning William was driven to the hospital in a state of high excitement with Prince Charles and Nanny Barnes. As soon as he arrived he ran along the corridor looking for Mummy. Diana heard the commotion and popped her head around the door, scooping William into her arms so she was holding him when he first saw his baby brother. Meanwhile Nanny Barnes was waiting politely outside in the corridor, anxious that the family should be left alone. After a few minutes Prince Charles beckoned her in to see Harry before she took a reluctant William back to Kensington Palace.

Once again Diana resolved to leave hospital as quickly as possible and at 2:30 p.m. on 16 September, dressed in a smart red coat, with her hair and make-up done, she was ready to face the photographers. Charles drove Diana and Harry back to Kensington Palace and then went to Smith's Lawn Polo

ABOVE LEFT: Prince Charles takes Prince William to St. Mary's Hospital to see his new baby brother, Harry.

ABOVE RIGHT: Princess Diana emerging from hospital with Prince Harry in her arms in September 1984.

Ground in Windsor Great Park, where he had a polo match organized. He was presented with a magnum of champagne by the opposing team and they held an impromptu party, using the back of a Land Rover as a makeshift bar. His polo-playing friends drank many toasts to the baby, already named Prince Henry Charles Albert David, to be known as Harry.

While Charles was playing polo Diana was showing her assembled staff the new baby back at Kensington Palace. Royal tradition dictates that the staff should see the new offspring, but naturally Diana did everything in a far more informal way than in the past. Instead of the servants lining up, she invited the two cooks, Mervyn Wycherley and Graham Newbold, dressers Evelyn Dagley and Valerie Gibbs, Francis the housekeeper and the new butler Harold Brown to have a drink in her sitting room.

In comparison to William's birth, Harry's arrival was less of an event – among the family at least. The Queen and Prince Philip, for instance, were in Scotland when they received the news they had become grandparents for the fourth time, but did not return until a week later. The Queen went and saw Harry as soon as she got back to Windsor, but it was several weeks before Prince Philip paid his grandson a visit. When asked, during the royal tour of Canada a few weeks later, he said that his busy schedule meant that he had not yet been able to see the baby.

To the world at large Charles and Diana were still the ultimate royal couple, and with an "heir and spare" their happiness appeared complete. Diana's modern approach to motherhood and habit of telling those she met little snippets about her children endeared her to millions, none of whom had any idea of the true situation. She claims that after the birth of Harry that something died inside her and her "marriage went down the drain." However, failing to come up to the expectations Diana had of a husband did not mean Charles was a hopeless father. He loved what Diana called "the nursery life" and as she only breastfed William for three weeks and Harry 11, he was able to help feed his young sons. "He couldn't wait to get back and do the bottle and everything. He was very good," Diana explained. "He always came back and fed the baby."

Charles's enthusiasm for fatherhood included his desire for his children to learn about the things he considered important in life. They were, after all, never going to have to make a living, and he decreed that the qualities of

BELOW: Nanny Barbara Barnes carrying Prince Harry down the aircraft steps after a visit to Balmoral in 1985.

patience and understanding were going to be far more important than being academic. "I would like to try and bring up our children to be well-mannered, to think of other people, to put themselves in other people's positions and to do unto others as they would have done to them," he said. "That way, even if they turn out not to be very bright or very qualified, at least if they have reasonable manners they will get so much further in life than if they did not have any at all." His ideology was similar to that of his grandmother's, the Queen Mother, who once told the actress Mia Farrow at a lunch party that she considered good manners to be the greatest asset any child or adult could have.

Baby Harry appeared to have these qualities in abundance and according to his father was "extraordinarily good, sleeps marvelously and eats well." This was in complete contrast to the boisterous William, who wanted to hold the baby all the time and cover him with kisses. With childlike cunning little William knew if he made a fuss of the baby, he himself would still be the centre of things. When he was not he flung his toys about and behaved in an attention-grabbing manner, as was demonstrated at Harry's christening at St. George's Chapel, Windsor on 21 December 1984.

The day started badly when William couldn't understand why he wasn't allowed to hold the baby as he had done during Snowdon's photo session some six weeks before. But Diana knew the delicate Honiton lace christening robe, which had survived for 143 years, would have been shredded if William had got his hands on it. She therefore turned to Lord Snowdon, who was taking the official photographs, for help. Snowdon came up with the perfect solution to keep William in the picture, but out of mischief – an antique birdcage, which held the excited little boy's attention just long enough for Snowdon and his assistant to get the pictures they needed. His assistant remembers being surprised by the attention William was getting from the assembled godparents and the Royal Family. "Every time he did something naughty they roared with laughter. No one admonished him and he was being a thorough pest."

William's antics were something of a relief to the Royal Family as formal photo sessions have a habit of being extremely stilted and he provided the distraction they all needed. The christening celebration was also being televised and shown as part of the Queen's Christmas broadcast that year. Naturally

ABOVE: Prince William holds baby Harry on a lace cushion in 1984.

OPPOSITE: Prince William with his mother, Princess Diana, holding baby Harry at the same photo call in 1984.

OVERLEAF: The Royal Family gather at the christening of Prince Harry on 21 December 1984: (*left–right, front row*) Lady Fermoy; HM Queen Elizabeth the Queen Mother; HM the Queen (with Prince William playing in front of her); the Princess of Wales, with infant Harry on her lap; the Prince of Wales; Frances Shand Kydd; (*left–right, back row*) Godparents Lady Sarah Armstrong-Jones; Bryan Organ; Gerald Ward and Prince Andrew; Prince Philip and Earl Spencer; Godparents Lady Cece Vesty and Mrs. William Bartholomew.

enough, Prince William's antics, including chasing his cousin Zara Phillips around the legs of the Archbishop of Canterbury, stole the show. In one sequence Diana is shown explaining to young William how many generations of the Royal Family had worn the valuable christening gown. "Great Granny was christened in it," she said. Diana had slipped up on her history as Palace officials explained later. "Great Granny's husband was christened in it. Granny wasn't." Great Granny was the Queen Mother who grew up to marry the Duke of York, who later became King George V, and it was he who wore the robe as a baby, as had several other royal babies before him.

Diana had more say in the choice of godparents for Harry than she had done for William. Her former roommate, Carolyn Pride, married to brewery heir William Bartholomew, was one and Lady Sarah Armstrong-Jones was another. Lady Cece Vesty, second wife of meat baron Lord Sam Vesty; Prince Andrew; artist Bryan Organ, whose informal portrait of Diana was vandalized in 1981, and old Etonian farmer, Gerald Ward completed the group.

Princess Anne was not there, claiming a prior arrangement to host a rabbit shoot at her Gloucestershire home. Diana didn't mind too much, however, as she had her sister Lady Jane Fellowes, whose daughter Laura had been born two years before William and son, Alexander a year later, and her mother, Mrs. Shand Kydd.

By this point Diana was well aware that the fairytale marriage she had entered into with so much hope was unravelling fast. She also had Nanny Barnes to contend with. The forestry worker's daughter had turned out to be a lot more independent and strong-willed than Diana had anticipated, and despite Barbara's loyalty and patience towards her boss, the two of them were soon at loggerheads. "Barbara guarded the top nursery floor like the Vatican," one of the Kensington Palace staff recalled. "It was her kingdom." Barbara was, however, wonderful with the children. She treated them as people and never talked down to them. If there were tears she diverted their attention to something else. And if the boys refused to put on the clothes she had chosen for them, she would divert their attention again and gently talk them around. She never went into head-on confrontation, but somehow always managed to get them to do what she wanted.

She had both William and Harry sitting up straight before their first birthdays, and they were taught to say "Please" and "Thank you" almost as

BELOW: Nanny Barbara Barnes takes William and Harry, in his stroller, for a winter walk through the park.

ABOVE & RIGHT: Prince William and Prince Harry pretend to play the piano in the salon of Kensington Palace in October 1985.

LEFT: Prince Harry at 13 months crawling swiftly in the salon of Kensington Palace in October 1985.

31

ABOVE: The Prince and Princess of Wales proudly hold Princes Harry and William on board the Royal Yacht *Britannia* at the end of an official trip to Venice in 1985.

OPPOSITE: Prince Harry on his first birthday on the deck of *Britannia* during the Western Isles cruise in August 1985. The picture was taken by Prince Andrew, who had recently taken up photography.

soon as they could talk. She would not allow them comfort blankets and refused to put their little feet into shoes until they had learned to walk properly. And when they did get their first pairs of footwear, she insisted on classic Start-rites with buttoned straps that were shaped to their feet. Sneakers were banned. Diana usually bowed to Barbara's greater experience, although she dressed them more informally and it had been her suggestion that the official photographs released to mark Harry's first birthday should be casual and relaxed.

They were taken by his uncle, Prince Andrew, while the Royal Family were on their annual cruise around the Western Isles of Scotland on board the Royal Yacht *Britannia*, and they showed the little Prince clutching a bucket and smiling happily. "They were taken as family snaps," Andrew explained. "I was just sitting on the deck, snapping away. If there was one that the Princess liked and one the Prince liked, then it would be used as a birthday photograph. They weren't looking for a formal portrait. I don't think it's fair on a one-year-old baby to have a formal portrait taken."

The formality Diana had set her face against was already starting to re-assert itself, however. On board the Royal Yacht, the Queen, concerned about the safety of her grandchildren, insisted that each had his own sailor to make sure he did not get into trouble or fall overboard. Diana dreaded these

33

family holidays where the boys had to be on their best behaviour all of the time.

Kensington Palace was still a lot more formal than a normal household and the boys were not allowed free run of the house and, as with Sandringham or Balmoral, their lives revolved around the nursery. That was the way it had to be and Diana realized that. It pleased her to see the Queen taking an interest in their welfare and fussing around their rooms, moving chairs and arranging toys. The Queen Mother, too, paid them attention when the fancy took her. She would tell them stories and sometimes hide their stuffed animals behind her back and ask playfully, "Where's teddy gone?" as they squealed with delight.

They were all enchanted by Harry, who never cried and only smiled. The troubles he would eventually have to face were still in the distant future.

OPPOSITE: Princess Diana holds Harry's hand tightly at Aberdeen Airport in 1986, en route to Balmoral to stay with the Queen.

BELOW: William and Harry playing on their rocking horses on the top nursery floor of Kensington Palace in October 1985.

CHAPTER THREE

❧ EARLY DAYS ❧

From the beginning Diana was determined to assert her authority in the upbringing of William and Harry. If she did not do so she knew she would lose her boys to a system she neither fully understood nor particularly liked. Whatever problems it might cause in terms of security, she knew they would benefit for the rest of their lives from mixing with ordinary children of their own age. The idea of having a governess, as both she and Charles had when they were young, was abhorrent to her and, after much deliberation and discussion, it was agreed that William and later Harry should attend Mrs. Mynors' Nursery School in Chepstow Villas, a quiet tree-lined street in West London.

Remembering the fuss that had ensued when Prince Charles arrived at his first school, Hill House in Knightsbridge, 29 years earlier, Buckingham Palace composed a joint letter from Charles and Diana to be sent to all the newspaper editors. The letter politely requested that after the initial photo call William was to be left alone. Mrs. Mynors did her bit too and spoke to the parents who had children at the £200-a-term school and explained that under no circumstances were any of them to speak to the press.

On a warm September day in 1985, 150 reporters and photographers waited behind crash barriers for the three-year-old Prince to arrive for his first day at school. William was used to cameras as he had been paraded in front of batteries of photographers on several occasions. But even for so sophisticated a youngster, it was a bit much and to ensure that he smiled for the cameras Diana had let William choose what he wanted to wear – a pair of red shorts and a checked shirt.

Throughout his three short years, media attention became commonplace to William and during his time at Mrs. Mynors' his classmates became as blasé as their rambunctious new friend. They took little notice of his armed bodyguard, who sat outside the classroom, or the banks of photographers who were allowed to photograph the tiny pupils returning from rehearsals of the school play. "His classmates hardly know who he is," Mrs. Mynors commented. "Sadly that won't be the case at the next school he goes to." Mrs. Mynors was not entirely right, however, and Wills (as he was nicknamed) had discovered how a bit of pulling

OPPOSITE: Princes William and Harry sit together on the steps of Highgrove House wearing their scaled-down army uniforms in July 1986.

FAR LEFT: Prince William leaves Mrs. Mynors' Nursery School in London with his bodyguard.

LEFT: Prince William leaving Mrs. Mynors' Nursery School after his first morning in 1985.

BELOW: Prince William with his parents being greeted by Mrs. Jane Mynors on his first day at nursery school in Chepstow Villas, Notting Hill Gate, London in 1985.

RIGHT: Prince William, on his way
to watch the Christmas school play,
is escorted across the road by a
teacher in December 1985.

BELOW: Prince William dressed as
a shepherd for the school nativity
play in December 1986.

rank enabled him to get what he wanted. "My daddy can beat up your daddy," he is reputed to have said. "My daddy's a real prince."

Traditionally royal offspring are trusted to behave themselves from an early age, but William's indiscretions, harmless enough for an ordinary child, weighed heavily against him. Diana was forced to slap his bottom in public on more than one occasion – something that would never happen today – and when he crept into a policeman's car at Highgrove to play with the radio telephone, Diana was very annoyed and gave him a sharp spank and made him apologize. In 1986 he had his first of many outings to the polo at Smith's Lawn, but from the moment he arrived he demanded attention. "Where's Papa..? Can I have a drink..? I want an ice cream…" Diana, who had arrived alone, found William's whining hard to deal with and was forced to bundle him into the car and take him straight back home to his nanny.

ABOVE: Princess Diana holding William's hand at a polo match at Smith's Lawn in 1986.

LEFT: Prince William on his Shetland pony, Smokey, being led by Diana across the fields at Highgrove in 1986.

OPPOSITE: Prince William saluting in Parachute Regiment uniform at Highgrove in 1986.

RIGHT: Prince William rides home in the carriage with Prince Andrew and his cousin, Laura Fellowes, after the wedding of Prince Andrew and Sarah Ferguson in 1986.

He was better behaved at the Service of Thanksgiving at St. George's Chapel, Windsor, to mark the Queen's sixtieth birthday, and only bobbed up and down in his pew, wide-eyed with wonder, as he looked to see who else was there. Three months later, when he was a page at the wedding of Prince Andrew and Sarah Ferguson, things did not go so well. Halfway through the ceremony boredom got the better of him and he fiddled and jiggled and played with his order of service, rolling it into a trumpet. He was hot in his itchy uniform – that of an 1846 Royal Navy sailor – and while it was thoroughly entertaining for the onlookers and the cameras in the abbey, the Queen was less amused. By the time she was a three-year-old child she had already learned to sit upright and still, when called to do so, and here was her grandson behaving as if he was in a playground. It may have been an old-fashioned view, but as the Queen observed, William was not as other boys and his behaviour therefore mattered more than it might in other children.

Charles tried to be the stricter of the two parents, but he was rarely able to sustain his irritation for very long and he loved nothing more than being with the boys in the gardens of Highgrove in Gloucestershire. There they could do as they wished and as soon as Harry was old enough to become his accomplice William taught him to terrorize the gardeners with slingshots loaded with little water bombs made out of plastic bags. Harry also liked dropping ice cubes down the backs of the household staff and together they ambushed guests at the gate, demanding money, and stuck their tongues out at the people on Charles's garden tours.

OPPOSITE: Prince William dressed as a pageboy, larks about with his cousin, Laura Fellowes, at the wedding of Prince Andrew and Sarah Ferguson in July 1986.

43

ABOVE: Harry dressed in a parachute regiment uniform showing a cut on the bridge of his nose from a fall in 1986.

RIGHT: Princess Diana carries Harry on her shoulders at Highgrove in July 1986.

OPPOSITE: Prince Harry learning to ride on Smokey on the grounds of Highgrove in 1986.

In common with many older siblings, William initially bossed his little brother around. He would order, "Don't do that Harry," or "Come here Harry – now." If Harry had a new toy, William would want it.

"William was the leader," a member of the staff recalled. "He was big and strong and Harry was the irritating, ineffectual little brother who was very much in his shadow." But as Harry started to find his feet he learned to give as good as he got, as younger brothers usually do. Small boys enjoy pitting their physical strength against each other and William and Harry were no different.

On weekends Diana took them to Cirencester, the local town, where they bought videos, ice cream and sweets. Often lunch would be an *al fresco* barbecue with the rest of the Highgrove staff. Charles did not join in as he felt awkward socializing with his staff, but he thought it was important that William and

LEFT: Princess Diana with Harry in 1986.

OPPOSITE: Princess Diana cuddling a tired Prince Harry at the Marivent Palace in Majorca in August 1986.

BELOW: The Prince and Princess of Wales, and the young Princes Harry and William, on holiday with Queen Sofia and King Juan Carlos of Spain in Majorca, August 1986.

ABOVE: Prince William on his first day at Wetherby School on 15 January 1987.

RIGHT: Prince Harry looks at photographers through his cardboard binoculars on his first day at Mrs. Mynors' School in September 1987.

OPPOSITE: The Prince and Princess of Wales with William and Harry and Tigger, their Jack Russell terrier, pose for their Christmas card in 1986.

Harry should learn to mingle with people from beyond the confines of the royal enclave.

Duly, on 16 September 1987, the day after he celebrated his third birthday with a visit to London Zoo in Regent's Park, Harry followed in William's footsteps and started at Mrs. Mynors' Nursery School. Accompanied by both parents and his brother, he was shy in front of the assembled photographers and when he left the school just before lunch he covered his face with a pair of home-made binoculars. Harry's first few terms at Mrs. Mynors' proved he was quite a different character from William. He hid shyly at break time and refused to join in the playground games that his brother had so often instigated. At first

he was embarrassed about going to the bathroom and wouldn't put his hand up to be "excused," and he felt overshadowed by the ever-present comparison with his brother. Psychologists explain that this is quite normal with a younger child who is dominated by an elder brother – in order to avoid failure the child tries not to do anything at all. But eventually Harry settled in and wasn't always longing to go home at the end of the morning.

Because of her own unhappy childhood, Diana was keenly attuned to her youngest son's delicate frame of mind. She knew Harry was destined to grow up in his brother's shadow and did everything she could to make him feel he was just as important as William. It was a battle she often fought alone, as the staff and other family members were inclined to fawn over William, just as they had done with Charles when he was a youngster. Diana understood Harry was always going to be the "spare" half of the "heir" equation and took great trouble to shield him from any lack of confidence he might suffer as a result. It was difficult. The Queen Mother would pat the seat next to hers and ask William to sit down, but paid Harry much less attention. When she died in 2002 William recalled with fondness the feelings he had for his great-grandmother. "It was a pleasure to sit next to her at lunch. She always had some great war stories and to hear them from her really brought it all to life, something that happened long before we were born." She was also an example to him as he explained: "Whenever I felt ill, I always used to remember that in the same circumstances she would battle on, no matter how she felt," he said. "She never gave up. I remember her as being a huge inspiration to me, someone to really look up to and admire. She was a historic link."

Diana quickly realized that although the little redheaded boy she called "my Spencer" was not so important as his elder brother, he was full of guts. He was fearless when he rode his little pony at weekends, as if he was born to be in the saddle. Shy he might have been, but it was not long before he began to cause as much havoc as William, who had started at his pre-prep school, Wetherby School in Notting Hill Gate in January 1987.

A month before, Nanny Barbara Barnes had taken off on a West Indian holiday to attend the birthday party of her former boss, Lord Glenconner, on the Caribbean island of Mustique. Here she hobnobbed with the likes of Princess Margaret, Raquel Welch, Mick Jagger and Jerry Hall. When a photograph showing Nanny Barnes socializing with these celebrities appeared

OPPOSITE: Prince Charles, Princess Diana and Prince William deliver Prince Harry to Mrs. Mynors' Nursery School on his first day on 16 September 1987.

people were intrigued. Why was the Waleses' nanny at this elite bash when she was supposed to be in charge of the heir to the heir? Charles asked himself the same question. He thought Barbara was too indulgent of William and he didn't like a member of his staff – however close – socializing with his circle of friends. It would have been unthinkable for Mabel Anderson, his old nanny, to mix with the "upstairs" set socially and he realized having a modern nanny had its problems. Charles grumbled, but he would never have done anything about it had Diana not become jealous of William's deep affection for "Baba," as he called Nanny Barnes.

When Barbara returned with her West Indies tan, she was aware of an increasing coolness between herself and her employers. William had completed 15 months at his nursery school and was ready for his next step, pre-prep school, where he would remain until he was eight. However much she loved her charges she was not going to stay somewhere she wasn't wanted, so she decided it was a good moment for her to leave. Immediately after New Year when Diana returned to London from Sandringham, Barbara discussed the situation with her. They agreed that William's first day at his new school, 15 January 1987, would be an ideal date to announce her departure. "I thought no one would notice," Diana confessed later, "but I was wrong wasn't I?"

Just how wrong she had been was revealed the day after William's arrival at his new school. The front of most of the newspapers were devoted to Nanny Barnes's departure and the inside pages to William's first day at Wetherby. Buckingham Palace refused to throw any light on the situation and merely stated that the move had been under discussion for ten days. Miss Barnes had no job to go to and no replacement had been found.

Royal nannies have historically underpinned the system and throughout the centuries royal children have been brought up not by their parents, but by the spinster daughters of policemen and forestry workers. It is the working-class nannies, not the royal mothers, who have assumed the responsibility for the nurturing and loving so essential for the emotional development of any child. It is the nannies who have been responsible for making sure that the youngsters in their care learn how to sit still, to say "Please" and "Thank you" and for curtailing any of the children's bad habits (both the Queen and Princess Margaret bit their nails as children). Most have been dedicated women who provided their royal charges with all the affection they required. But however

caring and competent they might have been, they could never compensate the lack of parental affection, which could occur as a result.

Diana broke the mould by insisting on providing the day-to-day care of her children and being around them whenever she could. "I want to bring them security," she said, explaining her approach to motherhood. "I hug my children to death and get into bed with them at night. I always feed them love and affection – it's so important." Her possessiveness sometimes bemused Charles, who was conditioned to put duty before family. It also made for a difficult situation with the nannies, as they were uncertain where the boundaries should be drawn and, instead of becoming part of the family, as tradition dictated, they came and went. After Barbara Barnes left, Diana "poached" Ruth Wallace from Prince and Princess Michael of Kent. Next was Jessie Webb, who had worked

ABOVE: The Queen, with Princes William and Harry, watch polo from the Royal Box at Smith's Lawn, Windsor in 1987.

53

for interior designer Nina Cambell for 15 years, and now works for Viscount Linley. Giving consistency to these domestic arrangements was Olga Powell, who had started as an under-nanny at the same time as Barbara Barnes. All were "old-fashioned" nannies in the sense that they subscribed to the notions of routine and order and of course the "Ps and Qs" and the general politeness of any well-brought-up child. Their presence also protected the boys from witnessing most of the problems in their parents' marriage – at the first sound of raised voices they were whisked away to the upstairs nursery.

The detectives, or personal protection officers as they are correctly called, also played their part. They were robust policemen, armed and trained in the martial arts and were destined to play a formative part in the lives of the young Princes. Wherever William and Harry went one or two of them was in attendance and naturally the boys admired and became close to them. Such was William's admiration for them that one day he declared, "I don't want to be King; I want to be a policeman."

They were not, however, surrogate fathers, as was often suggested. Charles and Diana had no intention of allowing their position to be usurped by their own bodyguards and in particular when Prince Charles was around, they made themselves scarce. Inspector Ken Wharfe, who started looking after the boys in 1987, said, "In terms of security it was essential to develop a good rapport with the boys and they had to trust completely whoever was looking after them." Nevertheless, because of their position, the detectives spent more time with the Princes than either Diana or Charles did, as they were both wrapped in their work. It was therefore left to the policeman to join in the boys' activities. When, for instance, Charles declined to take part in the fathers' race at the Wetherby sports day in 1988, Ken Wharfe took his place – and won, much to the boys' delight. And on holiday to the Isles of Scilly off the coast of Cornwall, it was the bodyguards who organized William and Harry's games of football and beach picnics. "They regarded us as jovial uncles," Wharfe said.

But no matter how hard the team around William and Harry tried to keep them in ignorance of their royal position it was simply an impossibility. The escort of personal protection officers, the palaces and castles, and the subservient attitude of those who came into contact with their parents made an impression on their young minds. As one member of staff pointed out, "There is nothing normal about those children – there is nothing normal about having two

OPPOSITE: Prince Harry dressed as a goblin for his nursery school Christmas play in 1987.

detectives and two backup cars wherever they go." Nor was that awareness to be entirely discouraged. However "ordinary" their parents might have wished their sons' childhoods to be, William and Harry were royal and the best way to learn how to deal with that was from the earliest possible age, as their mother's problems with adjusting to her situation had testified.

But if their future was unquestioned, the manner of their education was not. There was consultation with many people, including the Queen, on how William – a future king – and also Harry, should be educated. In the end, like most parents, Charles and Diana relied on recommendations from friends, and Wetherby School in Notting Hill Gate appeared perfect from every point of view.

ABOVE: Prince William (*far right*) gets set for his 100-metre race at his Wetherby School sports day in June 1989.

OPPOSITE: Prince Harry, accompanied by Prince William, arrives for his first day at Wetherby School in September 1989.

CHAPTER FOUR

❧ SCHOOLDAYS ❧

From the day Prince William arrived at Wetherby School in January 1987, and faced the now familiar battery of cameras, to the day he left almost three-and-a-half years later in July 1990, he was popular with his contemporaries. His emerging character had changed from boisterous toddler to a more caring mini-adolescent, full of physical energy. He was extremely polite – when he wanted to be – and when he sat around the table in the staff room at Highgrove, not only did he know everybody's names, but the names of their children and pets. Diana started to call him "my little old man" and staff observed how mature he appeared to be for his age. Wetherby's headmistress, Miss Blair-Turner, whose school placed great emphasis on manners and aimed to instil confidence and a sense of responsibility in the 120 boy pupils aged from four-and-a-half to nine, was impressed.

Having been taught to swim in the Buckingham Palace pool when he was still tiny, swimming was William's most proficient sport and when he was seven he won the Grunfield Cup, awarded to the boy with the best overall swimming style. Even at this young age he was showing an extremely competitive side to his character. He liked winning and for him simply taking part wasn't enough; furthermore at this stage of his development he still enjoyed being in the limelight. He had an aptitude for English and spelling and was musical, with a good singing voice that he displayed in several Christmas concerts, performing favourites such as "Little Donkey" and "Little Drummer Boy." It was the foundation of his appreciation and incredible knowledge of music of all kinds, which was to continue all his life.

Despite William's more adult behaviour, anything he did still made headline news, much to the distress of his parents. Two years after his much publicized arrival at Wetherby, he decided to relieve himself in a bush during a school sports outing at Richmond Athletic ground. Photographers were waiting and the following day a tabloid newspaper ran two photographs of William caught in the act. The headline ran "The Royal Wee Wee."

As a Wetherby mother rightly observed, William and Harry were always going to attract people's interest. But at least they escaped the isolation that

OPPOSITE: Diana takes Princes William and Harry to Wetherby School in September 1989. It was Harry's first day and they pose with headmistress Miss Blair Turner.

Charles had been forced to endure because of his princely position. It was Diana who broke down those barriers and allowed them to do the things that other children take for granted. She arranged to take them to McDonald's, to the spooky London Dungeon and to Harrods and Selfridges department stores to meet Father Christmas. Their holidays abroad however were less ordinary; they stayed with King Juan Carlos in Majorca, visited Sir Richard Branson's private island, Necker, in the British Virgin Islands, and learned to ski in Austria and Switzerland – followed as always by the ever-present photographers, there to record every adventure and possible misdemeanour, not only of the boys, but of their parents too as their relationship grew ever more strained. In 1988, when Prince Harry entered Great Ormond Street Hospital for an emergency hernia operation, Charles's absence was duly noted – he was on a painting trip to Italy.

The following September Harry followed William to Wetherby School. He arrived a week late due to a viral infection, but once there, he settled in quickly. There were no tears and no hiding away as had happened when he started nursery school.

ABOVE LEFT: Headmistress Miss Blair Turner says goodbye to William after his first day at Wetherby School in January 1987.

ABOVE RIGHT: Two-and-a-half years later, in September 1989, it's Harry's turn to shake the hand of the headmistress after his first day at Wetherby School.

LEFT: William holding an umbrella and Harry holding the hand of Nanny Ruth Wallace at a polo match at Cirencester in June 1987.

RIGHT: Cheeky Prince Harry sticks
out his tongue on the Buckingham
Palace balcony as he watches the
fly-past after the ceremony of
Trooping the Colour. William
is oblivious to what is going on
behind him.

BELOW: Prince Harry and Prince
William, wearing identical blue coats,
play on board the old-fashioned fire
engine at Sandringham in 1988.

LEFT: Princes William and Harry sit next to Prince Charles to watch the ceremony of Beat the Retreat at the Orangery, Kensington Palace, in June 1989. All things military are introduced to royal children from a very early age.

BELOW: Prince Harry as a pageboy with his cousins: Eleanor Fellowes (*left*), Alexander Fellowes (*centre-right*) and Emily McCorquodale (*right*), at the marriage of Charles Spencer and Victoria Lockwood in September 1989.

ABOVE LEFT: Prince William with his cousin, Zara Phillips, attending church on Christmas Day at Sandringham.

ABOVE RIGHT: Prince William taking part in a local gymkhana in Gloucestershire in 1989.

LEFT: Prince William, aged eight, and Prince Harry, aged six, riding on the Sandringham Estate, accompanied by a groom.

ABOVE: Prince Charles and Princess Diana accompany the two young princes for a bike ride during a break in the Isles of Scilly.

RIGHT: Prince William and Princess Diana meet the crowds as they leave Llandaff Cathedral in Wales after the St. David's Day service, March 1991.

ABOVE: A nervous Prince William, accompanied by the headmaster and his wife, arriving at Ludgrove School at the beginning of his first term in September 1990.

Four days before Harry's sixth birthday on 15 September 1990, a nervous William left home for the first time to start boarding at Ludgrove in Berkshire. In a show of family unity, Diana, who had driven William from London, met up with Charles, who had come straight from Highgrove, at the school gates. While the other new boys were taken to their dormitories, William had to suffer the embarrassment of shaking hands with the headmaster, Gerald Barber, and his wife Janet in front of the cameras. When they left William there and went their separate ways Diana was inconsolable. She felt she was abandoning him.

Once his parents had gone, however, and he had got over his initial bout of homesickness, William quickly settled into the routine of the all-boy school with its 180 pupils. His mother wrote to him every day addressing him as "my darling Wombat," but without access to radio, television or newspapers (it was before the advent of mobile phones) William was protected from much of the fallout of his parents' relationship and thrived in the protected environment. When the boys were at home on half-terms or holidays it was more difficult, however, and no matter how much Diana tried to shield them from the bad publicity surrounding the marriage it was impossible.

In the summer of 1991 William was accidentally struck on the head by a golf club and fell to the ground with blood pouring from his head. Transferred to the special brain unit at Great Ormond Street, it was discovered William had suffered a depressed fracture of the skull and needed an immediate operation. William quickly recovered from his injury, but the Waleses' marriage did not. It was fast approaching its denouement.

Just before the announcement of the separation on 9 December 1992 Diana made a point of driving to the school to tell William and Harry in advance.

William spent the next five years at Ludgrove developing a flair for English, soccer, tennis, cross-country running and of course swimming. He also proved he was a good shot and won the Cliddesden Salver for clay-pigeon shooting in 1994. He was secretary of the school dramatic society and appeared in almost all of the Christmas plays. Unlike Harry, William found the work fairly easy, and when he left in the summer of 1995 he passed the Common Entrance exam to Eton College with ease.

It wasn't so easy for Harry when he joined William at Ludgrove in September 1992. By this time, his parents' marriage was all but over and that summer Andrew

ABOVE, LEFT & RIGHT: Prince
William was a keen sportsman from
an early age. Here he is seen winning
the "cake race" at Wetherby School
sports day at the Richmond Athletic
Centre, and with Diana in a mother-
and-son tennis match at Ludgrove
School in 1995.

ABOVE: After Trooping the Colour Prince Harry is allowed a ride around the Buckingham Palace inner courtyard on his father's horse.

LEFT: Prince William runs off with the ball, as Prince Harry tackles his friends, while playing in the gardens of Kensington Palace in 1990.

ABOVE LEFT: Prince Charles and Prince Harry chat between chukkas at a polo match.

ABOVE RIGHT: Prince Harry holds the Queen Mother's hand after a Christmas Day service at Sandringham in 1991.

LEFT: Prince Harry sits next to Sarah, Duchess of York, at his seventh birthday party at Kensington Palace. Princess Diana, surrounded by Harry's cousins and friends, holds Princess Beatrice on her knee.

ABOVE: Princess Diana with Princes William and Harry on a chair lift during a ski holiday in Lech, Austria in 1991.

LEFT: Princess Diana, next to Nanny Jessie Webb and Princes William and Harry, on the Thunder River Ride at Thorpe Park theme park in 1991.

ABOVE: Prince Harry leads the way
accompanied by Prince William and
a cousin in Lech, Austria, in 1991.

Morton had published his book, *Diana: Her True Story*. Harry was, however, a happy-go-lucky fellow and, although he found academic work difficult and was sometimes inclined to be precocious and arrogant, he too settled down. Being good at sports always helps a child to integrate and although he was still in William's shadow, Harry excelled in that area and enjoyed Ludgrove, despite the tensions between his parents.

It wasn't to last and when Diana arrived at the school just a week before the official announcement to tell the boys she was separating from their father, ten-year-old William's emotional world fell apart. According to the parents of one of his contemporaries he changed from being a happy, open, chatty chap to an introverted adolescent. He buried his nose in books and spent hours wandering around the school grounds, his head bowed, looking as if he had the weight of the world on his shoulders. He also had Harry to look after and although the eight year-old acknowledged what was happening, he didn't fully understand until much later.

The Princes were taken on double the usual amount of holidays abroad, as each parent struggled to retain the boys' affection and provide a means of

OPPOSITE: Prince Harry larks about at Wetherby School sports day at Richmond Athletics Club in 1992.

LEFT: Prince Harry strikes a countryman's pose in his flat cap and Barbour jacket at Cirencester Polo Club in 1992.

escape from the upsetting situation. Diana took them on fun-filled trips to Nevis in the Caribbean, Paris, and Disney World in Florida and skiing in Lech. The trips with Charles were perceived as more stuffy, but to the boys they were just as much fun, and true to their royal pedigree the one place they loved to be was at Balmoral. There they could wander on the hills with their dogs, without any outside intrusion from tabloid photographers, who followed Diana wherever she went. Much to the Princess's irritation, Charles employed 30-year-old Tiggy Legge-Bourke, a family friend, as a companion-cum-nanny, whose upbeat approach to life provided just the distraction they needed. She was tactile, funny and a "good sport," and was happy to play soccer, ski or fish, and was a proficient enough shot to join the boys in the country pursuit they had grown to love.

After the separation, it was almost three years before the Waleses' first official family outing. On 7 May 1995, with William and Harry dressed in their

ABOVE: Princess Diana covers her face while Prince Harry yells with excitement after a soaking on the water ride at Thorpe Park in 1992.

LEFT & BELOW: Princess Diana, Prince Harry, Prince William and friends brave the log flume rides at theme parks Alton Towers, in 1994 (*left*), and Thorpe Park, in 1993 (*below*).

OPPOSITE: Prince Charles instructs Prince Harry in the rudiments of fly fishing with interesting results, during the filming of the documentary *Charles, the Private Man, the Public Role*.

ABOVE: Prince Charles, wearing a kilt of Balmoral Tartan, poses with Princes William and Harry during the filming of the documentary, which was directed by Christopher Martin in May 1994.

best, they travelled to London's Hyde Park to a ceremony commemorating the fiftieth anniversary of VE Day.

Three months later they were together again when they joined the Queen and the rest of the Royal Family in the Mall (the road that runs between Buckingham Palace and Trafalgar Square), to mark the fiftieth anniversary of VJ Day – victory in Japan and the end of the Second World War. That night there was great excitement as they were allowed to stay on board the Royal Yacht *Britannia* to watch a military flypast and a massive fireworks display. Their mother, who had been present for the London ceremony, was not with them.

It was against this disharmonious background with both their parents in new relationships – Charles with Camilla Parker Bowles and Diana with Captain James Hewitt and later art dealer Oliver Hoare, that William and Harry spent their formative adolescent years. It is much to their credit and the undoubted love of both parents that the boys developed as well as they did. Luckily they never lost respect for either of their parents and William, in particular, was

ABOVE: Despite being separated, the Prince and Princess of Wales got together with their sons for the VJ Day commemorative events in August 1995.

fascinated by his mother's "spiritual journey" with her New Age gurus and astrologers and her special genius for compassion. "Diana told Prince William more things than most mothers would have told their children," said her long-time friend Rosa Monckton, "but she had no choice. She wanted them to hear the truth from her, about her life and the people she was seeing and what they meant to her, rather than read a distorted, exaggerated and frequently untrue version in the tabloid press."

"The future Monarch was King William V and the Princess took none of her responsibilities more seriously than this – to prepare her children for life in the public eye," Patrick Jephson, her then private secretary said. Conversely Harry was the more adept of the two brothers at dealing with the media and his youthful self-importance enabled him to secretly enjoy the attention. According to Diana he "loved castles and soldiers" and the pomp of the monarchy, and both Diana and Charles delighted to indulge their youngest son's love of the military. When Harry was eight Diana took him with her on an official visit to Germany to see the Light Dragoons at their barracks at Bergen-Hohne. As Colonel-in-Chief of the regiment, Diana had to do the official "thing" while Harry had a wonderful time climbing in and out of tanks, watching mock battles and posing for endless photographs.

BELOW: Prince Harry wears camouflage paint as he rides in a light tank during a visit to the barracks of the Light Dragoons in Hanover, Germany in 1993. The Princess of Wales, who was with her son, was Colonel-in-Chief of the Regiment.

OPPOSITE: Prince Harry, who has always loved the military, enjoying his ride in a light tank in Germany.

ABOVE: Prince Harry, wearing a scaled-down uniform complete with his name, takes "orders" from a fellow soldier during the same visit in 1993.

They say that schooldays are among the happiest of our lives, but that certainly was not the case with William and Harry. Played out against the backdrop of drama and eventually tragedy, they had to carry on with their studies as best they could while trying to ignore what was going on around them. To some extent they succeeded, due in no small part to the attentions of William's, and later Harry's, Eton housemaster, Dr. Andrew Gailey of Manor House, who did what he could to shield the boys from the inevitable teasing and taunting of public school life. William got off to a difficult start as, on the day he arrived in September 1995 with both parents and Harry in tow, the

OPPOSITE: The Prince and Princess of Wales with William and Harry outside Manor House at Eton College with housemaster, Dr. Andrew Gailey on William's first day at school in September 1995.

PREVIOUS PAGE, LEFT & RIGHT:

Prince William, wearing the traditional Eton uniform of black tailcoat, striped trousers, waistcoat and white bow tie, which dates back to the death of George III in 1820, when the college went into mourning for the King.

front pages were picking over the revelation that the then England rugby captain, Will Carling, was the latest of his mother's admirers. William was a new boy in a school of 1,200 pupils where even the pedigree of a prince is treated with a haughty irreverence, and he was embarrassed and uncomfortable with the attention.

Both Diana and Charles had been united in their decision that William shouldn't follow in Charles's footsteps and go to Gordonstoun in Scotland. Charles had disliked it there, and although the Princes' cousins Peter and Zara Phillips both thrived at the unconventional – in some respects even progressive – independent school, it was decided that the next generation of princes would return to the traditional school where the nation's elite have been educated for centuries.

Large though Eton is, the two-dozen different houses where roughly 50 boys live provide a homey base that becomes the centre of their school life. They eat, sleep and study in house – joining the rest of the school for lessons, special studies and Chapel – which is obligatory three mornings a week. After lunch come games on the playing fields where the Duke of Wellington (a former pupil) reputedly said that The Battle of Waterloo was won. Much of the afternoon sport, especially soccer, is played in the house colours – in William's case, these were fawn and blue. In William's year there were nine new boys, each of whom had his own single room, and a study-cum-bedroom was also provided for William's protection officer. In this all-male and highly academic society the pressure is on from the start, which sometimes worked in William's favour, as it gave him much less time to dwell upon and worry about the problems that were besetting his parents. However the spotlight of attention made William the butt of a number of sly comments from some of the older boys. No young man in the throes of adolescence would welcome such attention and William was more sensitive than most.

At the beginning of the November of his first term Diana arrived at the school to tell her son about the forthcoming television interview she had done for *Panorama*, which was to be aired that very night. William watched the program in his housemaster's study and his reaction devastated Diana. He wouldn't speak to her afterwards and refused to take her telephone calls for the first time in his life. When he eventually came home to Kensington Palace all hell broke loose. He was furious that she hadn't told him she was going to do

it, furious that she had spoken badly of his father and furious that she had mentioned James Hewitt. He hated the idea of everything being on television and he knew his friends would poke fun at him, which they did. He felt she had made a fool of herself – and of him.

By the following morning his anger had subsided and he came into her bedroom and presented her with a bunch of flowers and made her promise that in future she would always tell him what was happening and what she was doing. That Christmas she asked William and Harry what they wanted and they said in unison that they wanted Mummy and Daddy to get back together. Diana burst into tears because that is what she wanted too, but events had already overtaken her, as the week before the Queen had written letters to both Diana and Charles demanding that they get a divorce.

ABOVE: Kim Knott was able to get Princess Diana looking very relaxed as she posed with Princes William and Harry. This picture was taken in December 1995 and was one of the last formal sittings of them together.

CHAPTER FIVE

❧ THE TEENAGE YEARS ❧

Delighted though the Queen was with William's progress at Eton she was worried about the various emotional pressures that were being heaped upon him. Under the Eton system the people charged with dealing with any troubles that William might encounter during his time there were his housemaster, Dr. Andrew Gailey, his dame (as Eton calls its matrons), Elizabeth Heathcote, and his tutor, C.A. Stuart-Clarke, and William was served by all three. There was only so much they could do, however, and they knew he was buckling under the pressure. "It was hard for him," one of his contemporaries recalled. "You wanted to feel sorry for him, but that didn't help as the last thing he seemed to want was people feeling sorry for him. He was very royal in that respect."

The one person who could help was the Queen. She knew only too well what pressures William was facing and told her advisors she was worried he might suffer in the same way as his mother had. Her natural inclination was to let the situation ride in the hope that somehow the problems would melt away, but Philip, ever vocal, pointed out this wasn't going to happen. He insisted that the situation Diana and Charles had created would have to be confronted and that the Queen would have to step in to help William, who, in turn, would help Harry.

On Sundays all the Eton boys are allowed out on the town. For William that came to involve a short walk with his detective, Graham Cracker, across the bridge to Windsor and up the hill to the castle. He would sometimes join the Queen and the Duke of Edinburgh for lunch, but afternoon tea was just for the Queen and her grandson, which they would take in the Oak Drawing Room overlooking the quadrangle. William would tell Granny what he had been up to and she would give him an account of what she had been doing and why. For much of his young life she had maintained a somewhat distant relationship with William, but the traumatic events of the previous few months had sharpened her focus and this most formal of ladies lowered the curtain of majesty to embrace him. She assured him that his

OPPOSITE: Here William poses for a series of photographs to celebrate his eighteenth birthday on 21 June 2000. As a sixth former and a prefect William could wear a non-regulation waistcoat.

mother was still held in the highest regard despite the removal of her HRH title and explained that the institution of the monarchy was something to be upheld and respected and was worth preserving. It was his birthright after all, as much as it was hers.

Despite her problems, Diana believed this too. "I wouldn't do anything to harm what is essentially part of William's heritage," she said, and added that she was determined that her elder son should grow up to appreciate the duties and responsibilities that came with his position. She was just as keen that Harry, too, should play his royal part in the future of the monarchy. "She was very conscious that both had a role to play," Diana's friend Rosa Monckton recalled. "She was grooming Prince Harry to be of support to his brother."

It was apparent however that anything Charles and Diana did together turned into a drama of sorts and, when, on 9 March 1997, 14-year-old William was confirmed by The Right Reverend Richard Chartres, the then Bishop of

BELOW: The Royal Family, in the White Drawing Room of Windsor Castle, on the day of William's confirmation. (*left–right, front*) Prince Harry; Diana, Princess of Wales; Prince William; the Prince of Wales; and the Queen. (*left–right, back*) Godparents King Constantine; Lady Susan Hussey; Princess Alexandra; the Duchess of Westminster; and Lord Romsey.

London, it was no different. Diana was furious about the inclusion of Tiggy on the guest list and refused to invite any of her own friends and family, including her mother, Mrs. Shand Kydd. Diana avoided talking to anyone she had previously employed and it took all William's willpower to overcome the embarrassing situation. He was nearly 15 and already six feet tall and was starting to exert his own authority: he was not going to have his day ruined by his mother's petulance. Harry, still only 12 years old, did not understand and kept asking "Where's Tiggy? Where's Granny Frances?"

Protected from much of the emotional fallout of his parents' marriage by his inability to fully comprehend the situation (he even asked, "Who's Camilla?" when he heard her name on television), Harry was enjoying his time at Ludgrove. He was an excellent horseman for his age, a good shot and a passable soccer player and cricketer. Academic flair however was not among his more notable gifts. Geography was a struggle and he used to be tested by his father on the world's capital cities and rivers during long car journeys. Mathematics was also something of a mystery, although in that he was only following in the tradition established by Charles, who needed three attempts before he passed his O-level in that subject.

Diana was determined that Harry should follow his brother to Eton. "If he doesn't go there everyone will think he is stupid," she told me. Harry wasn't stupid but he had learning difficulties in the form of dyslexia and

LEFT: Prince Harry, a keen fan of cricket, playing for Ludgrove School.

needed extra coaching in many subjects. It was decided that whatever happened he would stay at Ludgrove an extra year and hopefully manage to cram his way through the Eton Common Entrance.

As he became more independent William felt increasingly uncomfortable in the company of his parents because of the attention they inevitably attracted. During his first year at Eton British newspaper editors were asked to allow William total privacy and to a great degree they accepted this self-censorship throughout his five years at the school. When he was with his parents, however, he still attracted a great deal of unwanted attention. As a result, on Founder's Day in 1997, held to celebrate the birthday of King George III, and the high point of the Eton social calendar, he told them he did not want them to attend. The "fawning parents" as Diana called them, gather to picnic on the playing fields while their offspring go about their youthful business of chatting up their school-friend's sisters and a virtual army of their prettiest acquaintances. Instead of Diana, Tiggy and William's friend, William van Cutsem, were invited to join William for the afternoon's revelry.

When William returned home for the start of the summer holiday he found his mother in tears, upset that Tiggy had been invited and that she had been shunned by her own son. "What mother would like that situation?" she explained to me, and it was hard not to agree.

William had already taken two General Certificate of Secondary Education (GCSE) subjects – Latin and French – which he passed with A-star grades, taking eight more the following year, scoring a further A-star in biology, As in English Language, English Literature, Geography, History and Spanish and Bs in Math and additional French.

Despite her eventual £17-million divorce settlement (the divorce became official on 28 August 1996), and her various relationships, Diana was still very much loved by the public. She was able to use this goodwill to positive ends, and she remained committed to her good works. She realized the power of her presence and in the case of land mines, she travelled to the places concerned to see at first hand the true scale of the problem. But she also wanted to contribute in other ways – and it was William who showed her the best way of doing it.

In her determination to show her sons the harsher aspects of life outside the gilded circle, Diana had continued to take them to see the terminally ill in

LEFT: Tiggy Legge-Bourke and Prince Harry watch the Beaufort Hunt in Gloucestershire in 1997.

hospices and the dispossessed in shelters for the homeless. The visits had made a vivid impression, especially on William, who started to question the need for the opulence that continues to be a mark of royalty. During the Easter holidays when Diana took him and Harry to the Caribbean island of Barbuda for a break, he suggested to his mother that as she was no longer going to wear all her fancy frocks she should sell them for charity – adding that he should get ten per cent of the proceeds!

The sale was held in New York, four days after William's fifteenth birthday on 25 June 1997, and raised £1.86 million for the AIDS Crisis Trust and the Royal Marsden Hospital Cancer Fund. A fortnight earlier Diana had written to Mohamed Al Fayed, the Egyptian owner of Harrods and the Ritz in Paris, to accept his invitation for her and the boys to join him and his family in the South of France. Fayed had been very generous to her charities and another deciding factor was that he employed Raine Spencer, the stepmother Diana had once loathed, but was now very close to.

They arrived at the Saint Tropez villa on 11 July with the boys' two police bodyguards. Not only did they have the run of the villa but also the *Jonikal*, the £14-million yacht Fayed had bought the day after Diana accepted his invitation. The boys and Diana enjoyed the holiday and liked Dodi, Fayed's 42-year-old son, who was playful and fond of all the latest gadgets. What they didn't enjoy was the presence of so many photographers, who even chartered a helicopter to buzz over the villa. Diana became increasingly fractious and one morning took a boat out to the lurking press launch to admonish them for ruining her holiday. "William is freaked out," she shouted. "My sons are always urging me to live abroad to be less in the public eye and maybe that's what I should do – go and live abroad."

RIGHT: Princess Diana with Prince Harry on a jet ski during their last holiday together in Saint Tropez, France, in July 1997.

On Saturday 20 July William and Harry flew back to England, attended the Queen Mother's ninety-seventh birthday lunch at Clarence House and then joined the rest of the family for the last ever cruise of the Western Isles of Scotland on board the Royal Yacht *Britannia*. They then travelled with their father to Balmoral to join in the grouse shooting, which they loved, while their mother hopped between the UK and the Mediterranean. She kept in touch with the boys when she could get hold of them. "They're always out killing things," she said.

On 30 August William called his mother, who had just arrived in Paris, to tell her he was unhappy because he was being required by Buckingham Palace to "perform" at yet another photo call at Eton where he was to start his third year in four days' time. What troubled the Prince was the spotlight shining on him to the exclusion of Harry. Diana promised to sort it out when she returned home the following day. Tragically she never did.

BELOW: Prince Charles with Princes
William and Harry on the banks of the
River Dee at Balmoral in August 1997.
Two weeks later the boys' mother was
tragically killed in Paris.

ABOVE: Prince William by the River
Dee, throwing stones for Widgeon,
his black Labrador, August 1997.

RIGHT: On 6 September 1997
The Duke of Edinburgh, Prince
William, Earl Spencer, Prince
Harry and the Prince of Wales
follow the coffin of Diana,
Princess of Wales, to Westminster
Abbey for her funeral service.

When William and Harry were told of their mother's death on the morning of 31 August 1997, their emotional world collapsed. Numbed by shock they appeared calm and composed during the following week and on the day of the funeral itself when, as tradition dictates, they walked behind the funeral cortège. Their Uncle, Lord Spencer, objected to his nephews walking behind the gun carriage bearing their mother's body to Westminster Abbey, saying that he thought it was unfair, that they were too young, and that he didn't think Diana would have wanted it. William certainly didn't want it but Prince Philip persuaded him that it was something he might regret if he did not do it.

"It was just awful," Charles Spencer recalled. "It was something I would never wish on anyone. You could not look on either side, you were just walking through a tunnel of grief and it was a very odd feeling because you could feel the depth of the despair coming in waves on either side. I still have nightmares about that. I can hear the bridles and all the metalwork on the horses and their hooves and the wailing of the crowd. I have never been in such a nightmarish place in my life." He admired the way William and Harry conducted themselves. "I think it was an almost impossible task but they both did it brilliantly," he said. "I imagine they just blocked off what was going on around them and got on with it."

LEFT: The touching wreath on Diana, Princess of Wales's coffin, which is draped with the Royal Standard. The envelope simply says, in Harry's childish hand: "Mummy."

ABOVE: Prince Harry receives flowers from a mourner in the crowd outside Kensington Palace a few days before the funeral.

RIGHT: Prince Harry, head bowed in grief, accompanied by the Queen after the service in Westminster Abbey.

ABOVE LEFT: Prince Harry holds on to his father's hand as they look at floral tributes outside the gates of Balmoral Castle.

ABOVE RIGHT: Prince Harry and Prince Charles outside Sandringham Church, three months after the funeral.

LEFT: Royal business goes on – Prince William and Prince Harry attending a ceremony to launch the 16th Air Assault brigade.

ABOVE, LEFT & RIGHT: For Prince Harry's half-term break he accompanied his father to South Africa. Here they visit a Zulu village to watch a traditional ceremony (*right*) and make their hand prints for posterity (*left*).

On Wednesday 10 September, only four days after Diana's funeral, Charles took William back to Eton and Harry to Ludgrove. When William got back to his room in Gailey's house there were more than 600 letters waiting for him. Over half the school had written to him offering their condolences in a show of solidarity. The reaction that greeted Harry at Ludgrove was more circumspect. No one talked about it and newspapers and television were more carefully monitored than usual. It was Harry's thirteenth birthday on 15 September and his aunt, Lady Sarah McCorquodale stepped into the breach and joined Harry for tea, bringing with her the PlayStation game console that Diana had bought him in Paris.

To encourage Harry and to boost his confidence, his father took him on a tour of southern Africa on his first half-term break after Diana's death, with school friend Charlie Henderson and the ubiquitous Tiggy Legge-Bourke. Harry, his friend and Tiggy went game-spotting in the Botswana bush while Charles carried out his official duties. They met up in Pretoria where they were introduced to Nelson Mandela and were joined by the Spice Girls, who were on tour. Charles then took Harry to Rorke's Drift where, in 1879, 139 British soldiers withstood an attack by 4,000 Zulu warriors, winning 11 Victoria Crosses, a record unsurpassed for a single engagement. As often happens in the aftermath of the death of a parent, Harry was determined to do his best and he succeeded in passing his Common Entrance Exams in History, Science, English, French, Religious Education and trickiest of all, Geography and Mathematics.

BELOW: Prince Harry enjoys the company of the Spice Girls after their concert in Johannesburg. (*left–right*) Mel B (Scary), Emma (Baby) and Victoria (Posh).

OPPOSITE & ABOVE: Prince Harry smiles for photographers as he steps out in his Eton finery on his first day of lessons at Eton College in September 1998.

RIGHT: Prince Harry and his father looking at the Eton Register as Harry signs in on his first day.

On 3 September 1998 Harry joined Eton in Manor House – the same house as William. Always anxious not to overshadow his brother, William avoided the inevitable photo call and left Harry with Prince Charles to face the press. At 16 years old he wanted to be left alone to live his own life, sheltered from the glare of publicity. In a written sixteenth-birthday interview he admitted he did not feel comfortable with the adulation of screaming

OPPOSITE: Prince William seen captaining his house (Manor) in an inter-house soccer tournament at Eton in July 2000.

BELOW: Prince William playing water polo at Eton in June 2000. He was captain of the team and continued to play after he left school.

girls, which was not surprising. In November 1997 he had attended a lunch at the Royal Naval College in Greenwich and been greeted by some 600 swooning teenage girls, while the previous year he was mobbed on a visit to Vancouver's waterfront after a skiing holiday in British Columbia.

He admitted he was a keen sportsman and liked rugby, soccer, swimming, water polo and tennis. His ambition was to go on safari in Africa and see big game, and like all teenagers he liked music, particularly techno music, and loved fast food. He refused to comment on any particular groups; nor would he discuss his friends. His A-level subjects were History of Art, in which he eventually scored a B, and Geography and Biology, for which he received A and C grades respectively – enough to assure him a place at the university of his choice.

During his five years at Eton, William was a pretty good all-round student. Besides being an excellent swimmer and water polo player, in his final year he was elected to "Pop" – one of 21 self-elected elite of prefects who were allowed to wear fancy waistcoats. He also won the school cadet force's Sword of Honour, an excellent augur to the army career that he was planning.

OPPOSITE, TOP & BOTTOM:
Prince William prepares chicken
paella as part of the cooking course
in his General Studies program.

RIGHT: Prince William in a distinctive
waistcoat designed by tailor Tom Gilbey.
As a member of "Pop" he was allowed
to wear fancy waistcoats.

RIGHT: Prince William in front of
a computer at Eton in June 2000.

LEFT: Prince William walks down the Colonnade, near the main school entrance, wearing black tailcoat, waistcoat and sponge-bag trousers. He also wears a wing collar and white tie, a privilege for captains of houses and sports.

OPPOSITE: Prince William in the prefects' common room at Dr. Gailey's house at Eton, known as "the library."

Meanwhile Harry had settled well at Eton, although he was never quite as popular as his brother. Some masters called him "Wales." Others referred to him simply as Harry. Like William he joined the polo society and took a keen interest in soccer. He also had a mischievous sense of humour, which he was quite willing to deploy at his brother's expense. Well aware of his brother's aversion to being recognized, Harry took advantage of it for his own amusement and one occasion suddenly leapt out from behind a tree when William was taking part in a cross-country run to ask, "Can I have your autograph?" This led to a flurry of expletives from William, who complained that Harry had cost him his place among the front runners.

Always a prankster, Harry's devil-may-care attitude gave him a certain charm, but it also got him into a great deal of trouble outside of the restrictions of school. In common with many teenagers, he had developed a fondness for alcohol and smoking, and in the pubs around Highgrove there

BELOW: Prince Harry pulls out an opposing player from the "bully" as his team, the Oppidans, drew 0–0 with the Collegers in the annual St. Andrew's Day Eton Wall Game in November 2001.

LEFT: Prince Charles and Prince Harry battle for the ball during a charity polo match at Cirencester Park in June 2001.

LEFT: Another chukka and different horses, Prince Charles and Prince Harry during a polo match at Cirencester Park.

OPPOSITE: Prince Harry, photographed by Lord Snowdon to mark his sixteenth birthday on 15 September 2000.

ABOVE: Prince Harry as Conrade in a masked ball scene from the Eton College production of Shakespeare's *Much Ado About Nothing* in 2003.

ABOVE LEFT: Prince Harry on crutches attending the England vs. France rugby match at Twickenham in April 2001.

ABOVE RIGHT: Prince Harry is restrained by his detective, Leuan Jones, during a scuffle with photographers outside Pangaea nightclub in London in October 2004.

were several places that tolerated after-hours drinking. At the Duke of Westminster's grand dance in Cheshire in 2000 he drank so much that he was sick in the bushes and in Marbella in Spain he made a nuisance of himself by turning the golf course into a polo field, tearing up and down the fairways in his golf cart hacking the grass with his golf club as if it were a polo stick. On holiday in Rock in Cornwall he also incurred the wrath of the well-connected mothers of several girls for being rude to their daughters. Together with William he converted the cellars of Highgrove into a teenage den where they played loud music, and the two also dabbled with drugs in the bushes outside.

It was something that Prince Charles had always dreaded. "Drugs are something that worries me a great deal," he once told me. "They are so available. You can attempt to impose rules and regulations but they don't always work and my sons are especially vulnerable to being exposed or set up by the press."

Unfortunately, in January 2002 that is exactly what happened and the story of Harry's drugs shame was splashed across the front pages of the

News of The World, and went on to make headlines around the world. Harry was pulled out of school and driven to Highgrove where he was confronted by his father.

In an effort to limit the damage that had already been done, Charles revealed that he had taken Harry to a heroin clinic in South London to listen to addicts describe the misery they had endured as a result of taking drugs, and Harry escaped expulsion from Eton.

He struggled to pass his GCSEs and failed in two out of three of his first AS levels. His sporting prowess was, however, never in doubt, and he was House Captain of Games, and represented his school at rugby, cricket and polo. His philanthropic ideals were never in doubt either, as he displayed when just short of his eighteenth birthday he performed several royal engagements with homeless children and drug addicts, ending his day by visiting Great Ormond Street Hospital.

LEFT: Prince Harry meets 11-year-old leukemia patient Samantha Ledster during a visit to Great Ormond Street Hospital in September 2002. Samantha is handing him a handmade card for his eighteenth birthday.

ABOVE: Members of the Royal Family including Prince Charles, Prince Harry, Prince William, Peter Phillips and the Earl and Countess of Wessex share a joke as they watch a parade in the Mall as part of the Queen's Golden Jubilee celebrations in June 2002.

RIGHT: Prince William watches his brother help their father adjust his gloves as they leave St. Paul's Cathedral after the service of Thanksgiving to celebrate the Queen's Golden Jubilee.

RIGHT: Prince Harry rehearses for the Eton College Military Tattoo, where he was Parade Commander, in June 2003.

In an interview for his eighteenth birthday, William announced his intention to dedicate himself to carrying forward the good work his mother "didn't quite finish."

"Father is very happy about my plans," he explained. "He has encouraged me to take an interest in my mother's work." He admitted that he found the experience of his first solo visits both daunting and exciting, though he felt that he needed more practice. "It was quite difficult at first. I have seen my mother doing it so many times and she was so good at it. In the past I've always had my father and brother there. At things like the Queen's Golden Jubilee, when we met crowds in the Mall, I just followed what they did and shook hands as they did. But it's definitely harder doing things on your own."

Just before he left Eton, Harry was awarded the highest rank of Cadet Officer. He was only runner-up for the top accolade of Sword of Honour, which William had earned, but he was selected as Parade Commander at the Eton Tattoo in May 2003. There to watch him perform his duties was Tiggy

ABOVE: Prince Harry poses with some of his artworks during his final half at Eton College in May 2003.

RIGHT: Prince Harry in his rooms at Eton College, colourfully decorated with memorabilia from his trips abroad.

Pettifer, formerly Legge-Bourke, his erstwhile nanny, who was still an important presence in his life.

Five years at Britain's most famous school had brought about little obvious improvement in Harry's academic ability, although like his brother he displayed an aptitude for Art, eventually leaving with a B in that subject along with a D in Geography. His father said, "He has worked hard for these examinations and I am very pleased with the results."

Such results would not secure Harry a place in any university of repute and had he not been a prince, it is possible that he would not have had a chance to pursue his long-held ambition to join the army. Yet even in this high-tech new man's army Harry had much to offer, as the quality known as guts was something he had in abundance. He also had the physical confidence that his elder brother sometimes lacked and the determination he had inherited from his mother that meant if he really wanted something he was going to get it.

ABOVE: Prince Harry wearing Eton School dress. He is allowed to wear a wing collar and bow tie, called "stick-ups," because he is House Captain of Games.

CHAPTER SIX

✤ UNIVERSITY AND THE ARMY ✤

Both William and Harry teased their father that what they wanted to do when they left school was to become professional polo players. "I casually mentioned spending the year playing polo to him to see what his reaction would be," Harry recalled, smiling. William had already tried and had argued that a spell on the Pampas of Argentina was vital if he was ever going to achieve his ambition and become a high-goal player. The days when princes could behave like playboys and be applauded for it are long gone, however, and Prince Charles, failing to understand their humour, rejected the request out of hand, dismissing it as a "decadent throwback." He told William, and later Harry, that they had to use their time positively. They knew they had no choice but to fall in line with their father's wishes, but it didn't stop both boys playing polo in charity matches, both with and without their father, on the Highgrove team and also competitively for the army.

To William's surprise and considerable annoyance, as he disliked anyone trying to control his life, Charles invited a meeting of worthies to lunch at St. James's Palace to discuss his son's future, just as they had done 30 years before when Charles was a young man. Charles explained to his chosen advisors that while a year in Argentina was unacceptable, he did want his son to travel and meet people from different lands and backgrounds in order to gain the worldly knowledge that would prepare him for the lifetime of responsibility that lay ahead.

There was always time for fun, of course, and both William and Harry were devotees of the teenage holiday venue, Rock, in Cornwall. There in the company of other public school youngsters from well-heeled backgrounds, they got drunk, kissed girls and spent the days surfing and lazing around on the beaches. But for William it wasn't long before the work his father insisted should form an essential part of his gap year came

OPPOSITE: Prince William and Prince Harry play for the Highgrove Team at the Cirencester Park Polo Club in June 2002.

ABOVE: Prince Charles, Prince Harry and Prince William in their Highgrove team shirts during the presentation of the Gurkha Welfare Challenge Cup at the Cirencester Park Polo Club in July 2004. Prince Charles was aghast at his sons' tongue-in-cheek suggestion that they wanted to take a year out after school to take the sport up full-time.

LEFT: Prince William kisses model Claudia Schiffer, who presented him with a prize for winning at the Porcelanosa Challenge Cup Match at Ashe Park to raise funds for local youth charities.

ABOVE, LEFT & RIGHT: William and his cousin, Zara Phillips, on opposing teams, thrash it out during a charity bicycle polo match at Tidworth Polo Club in Wiltshire in July 2002.

LEFT: Prince Harry on the Eventers team and Prince William on the Jockeys team take a break during the match at Tidworth in Wiltshire.

ABOVE: Prince Charles supports Prince William at a photo call at Highgrove to announce plans for the first part of his gap year in September 2000.

into play and he flew to Belize to join the Welsh Guards on exercise in the jungles of Central America.

With the help of Mark Dyer, a former captain in the Welsh Guards, equerry to Prince Charles, and William and Harry's confidant, William's year was mapped out for him. He would be starting a degree course at St. Andrews in Scotland in September 2001, but in September 2000, accompanied by Dyer, he flew off for a month to Rodrigues, an island in the Indian Ocean, to study the conservation of endangered coral reefs.

Once home the anonymity he had so enjoyed was stripped away as he faced his first press conference at Highgrove, given as a thank you to the media for respecting his privacy while at Eton. William delivered a confident performance in front of the cameras and even answered questions about his mother's former private secretary, Patrick Jephson, whose recent controversial book gave an unfairly harsh account of his mother's mental state. "Harry and I are both quite upset about it," he said, "that our mother's trust has been betrayed and that, even now, she is still being exploited."

He went on to detail the remainder of his gap year, which was to be spent with Operation Raleigh in Chile. "I chose Chile because I had never been to South America before and I also wanted to go somewhere colder rather than hotter." He got what he wanted. The trip took him deep into Patagonia to the small logging town of Tortel where he slept with others in a makeshift dormitory in a wooden hut beside a river. "I was with a group of people I wouldn't normally be with and getting along with them was great fun and educational," he admitted afterwards. "There were some real characters in the group who didn't hold back any words at all."

For ten weeks William chopped logs, built a walkway, painted walls, entertained local children and even took his turn at cooking and cleaning a communal lavatory. He earned the respect of the other volunteers and kept them amused with his impressions of Ali G and his general bonhomie.

BELOW: Prince William making wooden rubbish bins for villagers at the team's accommodation in Tortel, Southern Chile, during his Raleigh International Expedition in December 2000.

ABOVE, LEFT & RIGHT: Prince William during his Operation Raleigh Expedition in Chile, chopping wood to erect a walkway to link the different parts of the village of Tortel.

OPPOSITE: Prince William entertains six-year-old Alejandro Heredia with a piggyback ride at the village nursery school in Tortel.

ABOVE: Prince William, who insisted on being called "Wills," varnishing the outside of the local radio station.

LEFT: The hard-hitting Prince undertakes construction work in the village.

LEFT: Prince William shows his skills as a DJ at the local radio station. William, wearing a blue fleece jacket, warmed to his role during the half-hour show.

LEFT: After a hard day, Prince William stretches out with a book in the team's accommodation, a drab nursery classroom jokingly known as Hotel Tortel.

RIGHT: Prince William, countryman, at the Duchy Home Farm in Gloucestershire in May 2004.

"Will is good fun," said Kevin Mullen, a young man from the crime-ridden View Park Estate outside Glasgow. "He is a real joker and popular with everyone." It was not all easy for William as he later explained: "You don't have any secrets. You share everything with everyone. I found it very difficult myself to start with because I am a very private person. But I learnt to deal with it."

When William returned home at Christmas, he spent a couple of months working on an organic dairy farm belonging to Simon Tomlinson, the father of one of his Etonian friends. Tomlinson, who owns the Beaufort Polo Club, is a countryman at heart, like Prince Charles, and loves country pursuits such as fox hunting and shooting. "It was the best part of my gap year," William said, "I got to see a completely different lifestyle."

It was the wild plains of Africa, however, that really captured William's imagination and for the last three months of his gap year he travelled to the game reserves of Kenya and Tanzania to learn about conservation – accompanied once again by Mark Dyer, who took time off from his work in the drink and pub retail trade to be with the Prince. Gap-year life for William was very different from that of his friends. After all, how many young men are accompanied on their travels by a police protection officer and a former Welsh

BELOW: Prince William on the pier at St. Andrews in Scotland. The Prince was two years into his four-year degree at the Scottish University.

ABOVE LEFT: Prince William browsing through the magazine rack of a St. Andrews newsstand for a publication on motorcycles in December 2003.

ABOVE RIGHT: Prince William out shopping in St. Andrews in Scotland. He admitted his workload had intensified but revealed he was glad to have switched courses from History of Art to Geography.

Guardsman? Furthermore, William's call to duty was never far away and he knew he could never escape his destiny. Now university beckoned and he wanted, in his own words, "to have some fun."

In the beginning that turned out to be much more difficult than he had envisaged. When William arrived at St. Andrews on 23 September 2002 and drew up to the ancient gates of St. Salvator's College with his father, there were over 2,000 onlookers plus a battery of cameras waiting for him. He had been spared the excess of screaming teenagers and near riot of bystanders that had greeted his father's arrival at Cambridge 35 years earlier, but nonetheless his welcome made him uncomfortable. He had chosen not to attend "Freshers' Week" because he was increasingly mindful of his responsibilities and was worried that he "might end up in the gutter completely wrecked." Unfortunately this earned him the reputation of being standoffish; in addition William was unsettled – unsure of the course he had chosen in History of Art and missing his former girlfriend, Arabella Musgrave, the daughter of the manager of the Cirencester Park Polo Club.

LEFT: Catherine Middleton, known as Kate, at the festival of British Eventing at Gatcombe Park in August 2005.

"I wasn't homesick," he said later, "I was more daunted." And at the end of his first term William turned to his father for help. "We chatted a lot and in the end we both realized – I definitely realized – that I had to come back," he explained. His decision had a lot to do with another first year student who lived just a staircase away from him – the glamorous Catherine Middleton. Her parents, a former airline pilot and air hostess, had cleverly turned their business acumen into a highly successful party accessory Internet business and put their three children through public school – in Kate's case Marlborough, where she excelled in both the spheres of academia and sport.

Kate and William kept bumping into each other, as they had formed friends from the same group of first year students, and soon started playing tennis together. Kate, five months older than William, had a boyfriend, but that didn't stop her becoming William's confidante and it was Kate who suggested he changed from History of Art to Geography, a subject he had always enjoyed. In turn he became supportive of her and in April 2002 paid £200 to get a front row seat at a charity fashion show to watch her strutting down the catwalk in a black lace dress over a bikini. A student tipped off the newspapers and Kate Middleton entered the public arena.

For the rest of their four-year university careers Kate and William remained close. In their second year they shared an apartment in a converted Victorian house in the centre of town with William's pal, Fergus Boyd, and when Kate eventually broke up with her boyfriend, William was there. Only his closest pals knew when his friendship with the leggy brunette with the cute dimples became something more, but it was clear that William was now thoroughly enjoying university. In a series of interviews designed to keep the media at bay he revealed how much he loved the freedom and space of St. Andrews. "I'm a country boy at heart," he said. "I love the buzz of towns and going out with friends and sitting and drinking and whatever – it's fun. But at the same time, I like space and freedom. I like cinemas, bars restaurants and lots of sport – on the beach, playing quick golf – just making use of everything up here."

William admitted when he first shared a house they were all very organized and had rotating duties. "We all get on very well, but of course it just broke down into complete chaos!" He also revealed that although he was not as fit

LEFT: Prince William and Kate Middleton at the Cheltenham Festival race meeting in March 2007.

LEFT: Prince William makes his water polo debut for the Scottish national university squad against Wales and Ireland in Cardiff in April 2004. His team lost both matches and were knocked out of the tournament.

LEFT: Prince William on the beach at St. Andrews in a wet suit preparing for another ride on the surf.

BELOW: Prince William (*centre*) and friends with surf boards on the beach at St. Andrews.

ABOVE: Kate Middleton in her graduation robes at the St. Andrews graduation ceremony in June 2005.

RIGHT: Prince William during the graduation ceremony. He got a 2:1 in Geography after four years studying for his Master of Arts.

as he had once been he still enjoyed playing water polo and was captain of the team, and he also played rugby and soccer and went to the gym. He was also teaching himself Swahili, which was proving a little harder than he imagined. "It's because of my love of Africa. I love the people of Africa and I'd like to know more about them."

At the beginning of his third year William moved into a farmhouse on a private estate 45 minutes by foot from the centre of town. He was joined there by his protection officer, two male friends and Kate Middleton. Before things got serious with Kate, William had enjoyed the attention of the girls who threw themselves at him and didn't mind who knew, but he guarded his true private life with something bordering on paranoia. He often spent weekends with Kate at the house he shared with Harry down a deer track from Birkhall on the Balmoral estate and went to extraordinary lengths to keep himself and anyone else close to him out of the public gaze. It was a measure of how attitudes within the Royal Family have changed that the future King was able to live under the same roof as the girl he was dating without causing uproar.

BELOW: Prince Harry, Prince William and Kate Middleton cheer on the England rugby union team during the RBS Six Nations Championship match between England and Italy at Twickenham in February 2007.

ABOVE: Prince Harry with his horse, Guardsman, in Tooloombilla, Australia, in 2003. Harry spent part of his gap year working as a jackaroo, herding cattle and mending fences on a ranch owned by friends of his late mother.

On 23 June 2005 a nervous William graduated in front of his father, stepmother and royal grandparents. He dutifully thanked them for coming and thanked the people of St. Andrews for allowing him the privacy he had requested during his time there. As he was to discover, it was the last bit of real privacy he was to have.

Harry and William have a fantastic brotherly bond and when things get tough they loyally stand up for each other. Along the way, their relationship has had its difficulties, of course, as all sibling relationships do, but when William returned from his gap year, Harry discovered that William's Etonian arrogance had gone and in its place was someone less judgmental and far less controlling. "We've grown up together and we have had to go through a lot of things together," William explained. "We've grown up around the same things and the same people and we'll always have that common bond."

William jokingly admitted that Harry had pinched all *his* ideas for his gap year, which seemed much more glamorous than his own had been. Indeed it was, and in September 2003 Harry flew to Australia for two months, where he worked as a jackaroo in Queensland and followed the England rugby team as they played in the World Cup. He returned home for Christmas and the following Spring of 2004, travelled to Lesotho in Southern Africa to work with children orphaned by AIDS. In doing this Prince Harry proved there was a more serious side to his character.

During his eight-week visit he made a television documentary, *The Forgotten Kingdom of Lesotho*, to highlight the plight of the children orphaned by AIDS. "I want to carry on my mother's legacy as much as I can," he said. "I don't want to take over from her because I never will… But I want to carry on her work… For most people, it's been a long time since she died – but not for me."

Diana certainly would have been proud of her youngest son's charity work and she would have been proud when, in September, he passed the

LEFT: Prince Harry holding the hand of four-year-old orphan Mutsu Potsane as they go off to plant a peach tree. Harry worked with children orphaned by AIDS in Lesotho, Southern Africa as part of his gap year.

ABOVE & LEFT: Prince Harry helps local people build a fence at the Mants'ase Children's Home near Mohale's Hoek, around 60 miles south of Maseru in Lesotho, Southern Africa, in March 2004.

LEFT: Prince Harry playing rugby with some of the children from the orphanage.

LEFT: Prince Harry meets up with his friend Mutsu Potsane during a return visit to Lesotho in April 2006. The Prince was there to launch his charity Sentebale, which means "forget me not," in memory of his mother, Diana, Princess of Wales.

BELOW: Prince Harry and Mutsu, aged six, inspect the peach tree they planted together on a previous visit Harry had made to the village in 2004 (see page 141).

ABOVE & LEFT: Prince Harry, making faces with Lintle and below with Mutsu during his return visit to the Mants'ase Children's Home in April 2006.

RIGHT: One of the first photographs made available to the media of Prince Harry's Zimbabwean-born girlfriend, Chelsy Davy, taken in 2003 while she was a pupil at Stowe School.

BELOW, LEFT & RIGHT: Prince Harry and Chelsy Davy watching the Cricket World Cup Super 8s match between England and Australia at the stadium in St. Peter's, Antigua during a short holiday together in April 2007.

tough selection exams for The Royal Military Academy at Sandhurst. Harry was delighted to have passed his four-day Regular Commissions Board Test. "I have set my sights on joining the army and I am really looking forward to going to Sandhurst next year," he said.

It was around this time that Harry reconnected with Chelsy Davy, an old acquaintance of his. Chelsy was born in Zimbabwe in October 1985, and had first met Prince Harry when she was a sixth former at the exclusive boarding school, Stowe, where they had friends in common. "I have known Harry since I was at school," she confirmed.

Their romance, however, didn't get going until they were reunited in a Cape Town nightspot during Prince Harry's gap year. Chelsy was certainly Harry's type. A bright, curvaceous, blonde who loves to party, she also has the trappings of wealth – an apartment in Cape Town, a sports car and a seemingly endless supply of international airline tickets. Her mother, Beverly, is a former Miss Coca-Cola Rhodesia and her father is multi-millionaire Charles Davy. In November 2004 Chelsy jetted off to Argentina to be with Harry during his six weeks on a polo farm and then in December there was a pre-Christmas family get-together on the remote island of Bazaruto, off Mozambique.

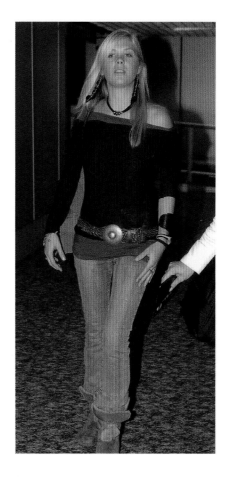

ABOVE: Chelsy Davy arriving at London's Heathrow airport on her way to visit Prince Harry in June 2005.

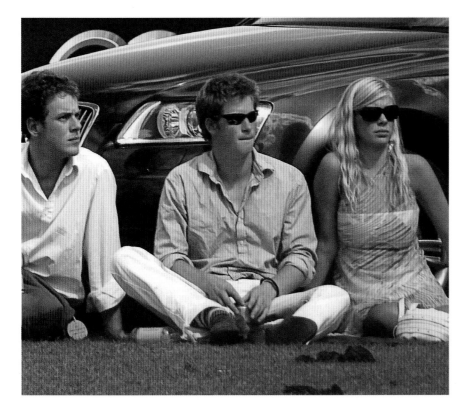

LEFT: Prince Harry, Chelsy Davy and a friend at the Cartier International Polo match at the Guards Polo Club in July 2006.

ABOVE: Chelsy Davy chats with Prince Harry during the Concert for Diana at Wembley Stadium in July 2007. The concert was held to mark what would have been Diana's forty-sixth birthday.

This jet-set romance was further fuelled in the following year when the young couple headed off to the Shakawe fishing lodge in Botswana for a week's safari, sleeping under the stars and going on dawn game drives. Unluckily for them photographers were hot on their heels and pursued them through the bush. Chelsy, who was by then studying Economics at the University of Cape Town, travelled to the UK to be with Harry as often as possible during his weekend breaks from Sandhurst. "Chelsy is cool," said a friend. "She loves to party and have a few drinks, but why shouldn't she? That is what we all do and if she was a studious, serious type, Harry wouldn't have been attracted to her in the first place."

In the past, the Royal Family have sometimes been criticized for not acting quickly enough in the wake of a disaster, but on the day after Christmas 2004, when the Tsunami disaster struck, they captured the public mood immediately. William and Harry pitched in to help the Red Cross relief effort and were both moved to tears by the desperate plight of the several million people who were affected by the tragedy.

Unfortunately their good works were eclipsed just a few days later when a photograph of Prince Harry wearing an imitation Nazi uniform was published. Although the Prince had been attending a private fancy dress party someone sold the picture to a newspaper and a global furore broke out. Harry issued a statement apologizing for his "insensitivity," but it raised the question of how he could have been so naive not to think of the possible consequences of his actions.

It was increasingly clear that Harry needed to learn how to come to terms with being a public person trying to lead a private life, and his upcoming army career, which began in May 2005, seemed to supply the solution that he was looking for.

On the whole, army life suited Harry, although for a while it is fair to say that he had his fair share of brushes with authority. He later admitted that it did him good: "Nobody's really supposed to love it [Sandhurst]," he said. "The first five weeks, the infamous first five weeks, are a bit of a struggle, but I got through."

On 12 April 2006 Harry finally completed his course and, watched by the Queen and Prince Philip, he took his place in Sandhurst's passing out

BELOW: Princes William and Harry posing with celebrity chef Gordon Ramsay before a charity run in aid of Sport Relief in July 2004.

ABOVE: Prince Harry marching with fellow cadets during the Sovereign's Parade at Sandhurst Military Academy in June 2005.

ceremony. He then became a 2nd Lieutenant – known as a Cornet – in the Blues and Royals, a division of the Household Cavalry, thus beginning his official life in the army.

Harry admitted that his two loves, apart from his girlfriend, were his army life and his charity work in South Africa, and instead of enjoying a lavish twenty-first birthday party, like Prince William's African-themed bash at Windsor Castle, Harry celebrated his birthday with another pilgrimage to Lesotho. Here he and his friend Prince Seeiso of Lesotho launched their own charity, Sentebale, in memory of the charitable work of their mothers. Both are second sons of a royal family and both had lost their mothers (tragically, in Seeiso's case, he has also lost his father). "I'm not going to be some person in the Royal Family who just finds a lame excuse to go abroad and do all sorts of sunny holidays," Harry said. He was determined that whatever direction his life eventually took, Lesotho and his charity would play a major part.

As heir presumptive, William's life was never going to be a simple as Harry's and while Harry pursued his army career William went on an 11-day visit to

New Zealand to support the British and Irish rugby team and carry out some public engagements.

The New Zealand tour was one of many firsts. It saw William perform his first ever solo engagement on behalf of the Queen, laying wreaths at war memorials in Wellington and Auckland to commemorate the end of the Second World War. He planted his first official tree, took his first royal salute, inspected his first guard of honour, conducted his first overseas walkabout, made his first public hospital visit – all of them staples of the Court Circular and a taste of his life to come. The verdict from all those that met him was the same – he had what it takes.

In January 2006 having gained an understanding of finance through carefully chosen work experience, followed by the contrast of two weeks spent with the RAF's Mountain Rescue Team in North Wales, William joined Harry at the Royal Military Academy Sandhurst to begin his 44 weeks of training to

BELOW: Prince Harry cannot help but smile when he is inspected by his proud grandmother, the Queen, during his passing out Sovereign's Parade at Sandhurst Military Academy in April 2006.

be an army officer. Their time at the college overlapped by four months, but for once Harry had got there first.

On 15 December 2006, watched by girlfriend Kate Middleton and her parents, William took part in *his* official passing out parade. Kate's presence at the Sovereign's Parade overshadowed that of Prince Charles and Camilla, and even the Queen herself, and provoked much speculation about a possible marriage at some point in the future.

William and Kate have known each other since September 2001 and have been dating, with a couple of breaks, for almost as long. The Prince has his myriad commitments, but whether the tragic events that have shaped the lives of himself and his younger brother have affected their attitudes towards marriage, we can only wait and see.

ABOVE: Prince William being greeted with a *hongi*, the traditional Maori welcome, during a visit to the Starship Children's Hospital in Auckland, New Zealand, in 2005.

OPPOSITE: Prince William smiles as he is inspected by his grandmother, the Queen, during his passing out Sovereign's Parade at the Royal Military Academy, Sandhurst, in December 2006, eight months after Prince Harry.

OPPOSITE: Kate Middleton with her mother, Carole, and father, Michael, at Prince William's passing out Sovereign's Parade at the Royal Military Academy, Sandhurst, in December 2006.

RIGHT: Prince William lays a wreath at the Cenotaph in November 2007. This was the first time that he had performed this duty during the annual ceremony to commemorate Britain's war dead.

CHAPTER SEVEN

❦ FINE YOUNG MEN ❦

As a young man Prince Charles's career was mapped out for years ahead, his friends vetted and his activities carefully chaperoned. He hated it and according to Diana, it stunted his emotional growth. She was determined this would not happen to her sons. Nor has it. Harry has been allowed to run free in a way that would have been unthinkable even a generation ago. He has also been able to serve his country in a war zone. Although this will be denied to William, he has to a large extent been given the licence to make his own arrangements.

This is how Diana would have wished it. Indeed it is how she insisted they should be brought up. She understood how much William in particular hated the publicity he attracted, but explained to him that he would just have to learn to live with it and that he would find it easier as he matured. As the focus of global attention, however, William and Harry have had more to put up with than Diana ever would have envisaged.

The initial trauma of their mother's death was followed by the French judicial investigation, which lasted seven years, the Metropolitan Police inquiry "Operation Paget," then the six-month-long inquest held in the Royal Courts of Justice in London. The verdict, which was eventually delivered in April 2008, was of unlawful killing attributed to the "grossly negligent driving of the following vehicles and the Mercedes." Finally, ten-and-a-half years after Diana's death, it was all over. William and Harry put out a joint statement thanking the jury, the coroner, Lord Justice Scott Baker, and in particular Trevor Rees, the only survivor of the crash. "Finally," they said, "the two of us would like to express our most profound gratitude to all those who fought so desperately to save our mother's life on that tragic night."

Over the decade since Diana's death, the two Princes had been forced on the defensive, forever on guard to defend their mother's reputation. They had resented the way their mother's follies and foibles kept being dredged up in a way which they thought betrayed her memory. Time and time again they had to come to the public defence of her good name. The drip feed of intimate, and to the Princes' way of thinking, unconscionable revelations from her former staff began with her private secretary Patrick Jephson. This was followed by the publication of a book

OPPOSITE: Princes William and Harry wearing army mufti of regimental ties, bowler hats, and carrying furled umbrellas for the annual Combined Cavalry Old Comrades Association Parade in Hyde Park in May 2007. This was the eighty-third anniversary of the unveiling and dedication of the memorial in the park.

ABOVE: Prince Harry and Prince William before the Concert for Diana at the new Wembley Stadium at the end of June 2007.

by their former protection officer, Ken Wharfe, but worst of all was butler Paul Burrell's revelations published in 2003, after the collapse of his trial on charges that he had allegedly stolen items belonging to Princess Diana. William was particularly incensed, accusing him of "cold and overt betrayal." To Burrell's claim that he had only written the book because it was what Diana would have wanted, William retorted, "It is not only deeply painful for the two of us, but also for everyone else affected, and it would mortify our mother if she were alive today."

To prevent further hijacking of their mother's memory, they decided to orchestrate the tenth anniversary of her death themselves. "We both wanted to put *our* stamp on it," William said firmly in the first of a series of interviews. "We want it to represent exactly what our mother would have wanted." Together the Princes decided on a concert "full of energy" that would include the artists their mother loved, on what would have been her forty-sixth birthday, followed by a memorial service on 31 August, the anniversary of her death. Their own charities, Centrepoint and Sentebale, would benefit, along with the other five organizations of which the Princess was Patron at the time of her death. The Concert for Diana, as it was called, would take place at the new Wembley Stadium. As both Princes were army officers in the Blues and Royals, the memorial service was scheduled to take place at the Guards Chapel at Wellington Barracks in London.

For the next six months, between their army commitments, both boys set about using their influence to secure the acts they wanted, which included Sir Elton John, Rod Stewart, The English National Ballet and dozens of others. To promote the concert they agreed to conduct a series of interviews from their home, Clarence House, to talk about their lives, the concert, their mother, and what she meant to them.

They were a good double-act, both self-deprecating and funny, yet honest about their feelings. When questioned about their mother they admitted that they never stopped wondering exactly how she had died, but dismissed all the conspiracy theories as unbelievable. When asked about their childhood William said he had been given the nickname "Wombat" when his parents travelled with him to Australia which had kind of "stuck" with him, while Harry was called "Ginger" by his friends. In answer to questions about Kate Middleton, with whom William had recently split up (the interviews were conducted three months before the concert), he showed remarkable diplomacy. "What I do with my private life is really between me and myself basically," he said firmly. "I don't listen to newspapers. Let them write what they want. Because you can't stop it and there is no point fighting it."

At the time of the interview Harry believed he was on the verge of deploying to Iraq with his regiment and his determination to fight for his country was the subject of enormous controversy as he was such a high-value target. Jihadist websites were literally calling for his head and many believed his presence was likely to be too much of a risk for his own men. A few weeks later the Ministry of Defence decided against deploying him and Harry had to wait until the end of the year to get his taste of real action.

Just after 4 p.m. on 1 July 2007, William and Harry stood on stage at Wembley in front of a cheering crowd of 63,000 music fans and a global television audience of 165 million people in 140 countries. Harry spoke first, uttering the greeting, "Hello Wembley!" to huge cheers. Looking slightly nervous, the Princes then took

ABOVE: Kate Middleton, dressed stylishly, walking to the parade ring during the Cheltenham Races in March 2007.

ABOVE: Prince Harry gives the opening address at the Concert for Diana from the stage at Wembley Stadium in July 2007. The Princes took turns speaking to the huge crowd.

it in turns to speak, referring to cue cards in the palms of their hands from time to time. "I'd just like to tell you why we're all here tonight," said William. "This evening is about all that our mother loved in life: her music, her dance, her charities, and her family and friends." Sir Elton John then kicked off the show with a rendition of "Your Song" in front of a giant black-and-white photograph of Diana. For once a concert that would usually feel disjointed with incongruous acts such as P Diddy, Duran Duran, Joss Stone and Take That in the same line-up, actually felt like it had a purpose. It was a phenomenal gig in honour of a woman who didn't do what people expected of her, hosted with great style by her two sons, who didn't always do what people expected of them.

LEFT: Princes
William and
Harry thank the
crowd and the
performing artists
after the charity
Concert for Diana.

A month later on 31 August, the anniversary of Diana's death, Prince Charles and his two sons personally greeted many of the 500-strong congregation made up of family, friends, former employees and representatives of various charities at the Guards Chapel. They were all there with one purpose – to remember the woman forever known as "The People's Princess."

It was a traditional church service with powerful choral anthems, uplifting hymns and reflective prayers. But it was Prince Harry's emotional tribute to "the best mother in the world" that proved to be the most moving commemoration. Nervous, but determined to do justice to her memory and share with the world the words he had written himself, the Prince stepped up to the lectern. "William and I can separate our life into two parts," he began. "There were those years when we were blessed with the physical presence beside us of both our mother and father. And then there are the ten years since our mother's death." His voice appeared to catch as he went on to speak about the Princess's unrivalled love of life. But loudly and clearly he continued, despite

BELOW: Prince Harry chats with his uncle, Lord Spencer, and aunt, Lady Sarah McCorquodale, after the service to celebrate the life of Diana, Princess of Wales at the Guards Chapel on 31 August 2007.

the knowledge that a mass worldwide television audience was watching. He spoke about Diana's "amazing public work," and how she was his and William's guardian, friend and protector. "But behind the media glare, to us, just two loving children, she was quite simply the best mother in the world."

Harry called for the Princess to be remembered in the way she would have wanted. "It was an event which changed our lives forever, as it must have done for everybody who lost someone that night," he said. "But what is far more important to us now, and into the future, is that we remember our mother as she would have wished to be remembered – as she was: fun-loving, generous, down-to-earth and genuine. We both think of her every day. We speak about her and laugh together at the memories. Put simply, she made us and so many other people happy. May this be the way that she is remembered." The Princess's favourite hymn, "I Vow to Thee My Country," played her wedding and her funeral, was the rejoicing finale. Diana's sons – her greatest legacy – had done her proud.

The absence of Camilla Parker Bowles from the service had caused some tension. Prince Charles obviously wanted his wife to attend, but it was always going to be an uncomfortable situation. At the last minute, with the personal backing of the Queen, Camilla tactfully decided to opt out, and took a holiday with some girlfriends instead. Prince William and Prince Harry had no objections

ABOVE: Prince Charles, Prince Harry and Prince William wait to greet guests outside the Guards Chapel before the service in memory of Diana, Princess of Wales.

to the presence of Camilla. Despite their mother's understandable animosity and the claims that Camilla had ruined her marriage, they bore her no grudge. She wasn't pushy, she did not interfere in their lives and, best of all, she made their father happy. So many of their friends came from broken homes that it was nothing abnormal to them to have a stepmother and get along with her, whatever some press reports have claimed.

When Harry gave an interview for his twenty-first birthday he described his father as "much more relaxed" since he married Camilla in April 2005 in the Guildhall in Windsor. William and Harry actually let out a whoop of delight when the couple exchanged their wedding vows. After the wedding breakfast William, Harry and Camilla's son Tom Parker Bowles cheekily decorated the royal car and

ABOVE: The Clarence House official photo of the Prince of Wales and his new bride, the Duchess of Cornwall, with their families: (*left–right, back row*) Prince Harry; Prince William; Tom Parker Bowles; Laura Parker Bowles; (*left–right, front row*) The Duke of Edinburgh; HM the Queen; and Camilla's father, Major Bruce Shand. They are in the White Drawing room at Windsor Castle in April 2005.

raced across the grass to be the last to see the honeymooners out of the gate.

"To be honest with you," Harry said, "she's always been very close to me and William. But no, she's not the wicked stepmother. Everyone has to understand it's very hard for her. Look at the position she's coming into. Don't feel sorry for me and William, feel sorry for her. We're very happy to have her around."

BELOW: The Queen's eightieth birthday dinner at Clarence House: (*left–right, back row*) Timothy Laurence; Peter Phillips; Daniel Chatto; Sarah Chatto; Prince Michael; Princess Michael; The Duke of Kent, Princess Alexandra; Viscount Linley; Viscountess Linley; the Duchess of Gloucester; the Duke of Gloucester; (*left–right, middle row*) Princess Anne; Autumn Kelly; Zara Phillips; Princess Beatrice; Prince Andrew; Princess Eugenie; the Earl of Wessex; the Countess of Wessex. (*left–right, front row*) Prince William; Prince Charles; HM the Queen; Prince Philip; the Duchess of Cornwall; Prince Harry.

On 14 December 2007, amid great secrecy, Harry got his wish and was deployed to the front line in Afghanistan two months after his regiment, The Blues and Royals, arrived there. The Ministry of Defence had been working closely with the British press for months beforehand to find a way to allow the young Prince to realize his ambition. His presence went unreported until the Australian magazine, *New Idea*, leaked the news in January. When it was then carried on the major American website, the *Drudge Report*, a month later, army bosses were forced to order an instant extradition, pulling Harry out to ensure both his safety and that of the soldiers around him. As he returned to the military airbase in Brize Norton, Oxfordshire, photographs and interviews were released as the army's part of the bargain. Although disappointed to have to return more than a month before the rest of his regiment, Harry realized that he had been fortunate to be able to go at all. For once the British media had come out looking good.

OPPOSITE: Prince Harry, in his desert warfare uniform, speaks out at a press conference at Brize Norton airbase in Oxfordshire immediately after he had arrived back from Afghanistan. Looking back at his time on the front line, Harry said that he had enjoyed the relative anonymity and the chance it had given him to be "one of the lads."

ABOVE: Prince Harry listening to a briefing before going out on patrol during his ten weeks on the front line in Helmand Province in January 2008.

RIGHT: Prince Harry takes cover in a ruined building in the deserted town of Garmsir, close to the Forward Operating Base.

ABOVE: Prince Harry, who enjoyed total anonymity during his deployment to Afghanistan, glances at a local resident astride a tiny donkey.

RIGHT: Prince Harry, known only as Widow Six Seven, talks to aircraft operating over Afghanistan. He compared his role in organizing air strikes to that of an air-traffic controller.

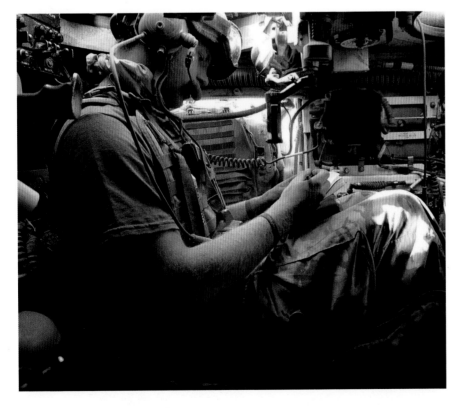

ABOVE: Prince Harry's battle group in the desert of Southern Afghanistan: (*left–right*) Lance Corporal Frankie O'Leary; Corporal of the Horse Paul Carrington; Prince Harry (Cornet Wales); Lance Corporal Chris Douglass; Lance Corporal Steve "Gerri" Halliwell; (*left–right, kneeling*) Trooper Jale Galavakadua; Trooper Max Matai Loloma.

LEFT: Sitting below the turret of his Spartan armoured vehicle the 23-year-old Household Cavalry officer, known as "Ginge" to his friends, communicates with other units by radio. Prince Harry said that his time in Afghanistan was one of the happiest of his life.

LEFT: Prince Harry larks about on a small motorcycle beside two armoured vehicles draped with camouflage netting.

BELOW: Prince Harry in position, his goggles on. Second Lieutenant Wales in C squadron of the Household Cavalry was heading a convoy of light tanks.

OPPOSITE: Prince Harry on patrol through the deserted town of Garmsir during his deployment to Afghanistan in February 2008.

RIGHT: Prince Harry sits with his fellow soldiers in an area of the observation post on JTAC Hill, eating peanuts. The food was nourishing, but monotonous, with goat stew, pasta and bologna sauce and curries being the nightly fare.

BELOW: Prince Harry chats with a Ghurkha after firing a 50mm machine gun at Taliban fighters from the observation post at JTAC Hill.

ABOVE: Stripped to the waist, Prince Harry shows off his skills with a rugby ball during a break in duties in the desert of Helmand Province.

LEFT: Prince Harry sitting inside the Fire Planning Cell close to forward operating base in Helmand Province.

Harry spoke of how his deployment offered him a level of anonymity he had never before experienced and said that when he was initially refused permission to serve in Iraq he wished he was not a prince. "I wish that quite a lot actually," he said poignantly. "It's very nice to be a normal person for once. I think this is about as normal as I am ever going to get. This is what it's all about, being here with the guys rather than being in a room with a bunch of officers," he said. "All my wishes have come true; I managed to get the job done. And no, I don't miss the booze, if that's the next question." He added quickly. "It's just nice to be here with all the guys and just mucking in as one of the lads."

OPPOSITE: A disappointed Prince Harry arriving back from Afghanistan at Brize Norton airbase in Oxfordshire.

ABOVE: After a press conference at the airbase Prince Harry, accompanied by Prince William and Prince Charles, heads home to Highgrove for a well-earned lunch in February 2008.

William, meanwhile, was following in his father's footsteps by learning to pilot helicopters and fixed-wing aircraft during a four-month secondment with the RAF at Cranwell in Lincolnshire. The secondment allowed him to realize a lifetime's ambition to fly – even as a little boy William would clamber on board royal helicopters and pretend to fly them, and he loved being allowed to join his father when Prince Charles inspected members of the Parachute Regiment at Highgrove.

In April 2008, watched by his girlfriend, Kate – her first appearance at a formal event since 2006 – he received his "wings" from Prince Charles, who holds the rank of Air Chief Marshal, at the graduation ceremony. He thus became the fourth successive generation of the monarchy to become an RAF pilot. His father and his grandfather, the Duke of Edinburgh, both earned the RAF flying badge, while his great-grandfather, Prince Albert, later King George VI, served in the RAF between 1918 and 1919, the first royal to do so. As with the RAF, Prince William was then attached to the Royal Navy, gaining understanding of the fullest spectrum of the navy's capabilities – from submarines to the ships of the surface fleet, as well as the Fleet Air Arm. His stint in the forces is, however, only a prelude to his one day becoming Head of the Armed Forces and a full-time working member of the Royal Family.

William and Harry are immensely privileged, rich young men who will never have to worry about the problems of everyday life. They have another problem, however, which to be fair, might appear far worse to them: the loss of their freedom to be their real selves. They want to enjoy themselves and be one of the crowd sometimes, but sadly for them, because of an accident of birth they are not and never will be. The normality that Diana, Princess of Wales, attempted to give them in abundance by taking them around with her to see the harsher side of life, is an almost impossible objective, as she discovered.

How can they be normal when they see themselves in newspapers and on television almost every day and observe the obsequious manner in which powerful people approach them? Moral judgements will always be made and the judgements the Princes face on the issue of partying and drinking, which have sometimes caused problems, depend to a greater extent on the age group judging them. Their peers find nothing wrong with their behaviour, but older people find it disrespectful and loutish because that is not what they expect from their Royal Family. The Princes, if judged by the relaxed standards of today, are

OPPOSITE: Prince Charles, in his role as Air Chief Marshal, congratulates his son, Prince William. Prince Charles had just presented him with his wings, following his graduation ceremony at RAF Cranwell in Lincolnshire in April 2008.

RIGHT: Prince William and Kate Middleton, who said her boyfriend "looked gorgeous," head off to lunch after the presentation. The Prince learned to fly as part of a four-month attachment with the RAF.

ABOVE & LEFT: Flying Officer William Wales on his first day of training at Cranwell, Lincolnshire, four months earlier.

OPPOSITE: As President of the UK's Football Association, Prince William, wearing his trademark odd socks, discusses tactics with his junior team from Centrepoint. The youngsters were taking part in a course at Westgate Community College, Newcastle, in October 2007.

LEFT: Prince William joins in the five-a-side junior tournament playing in defence for his team.

BELOW: Prince William adopting the bended-knee stance so reminiscent of his late mother, while talking to schoolchildren during a visit to the Valley Children's Project in the Rhonda Valley, Wales, in May 2008.

ABOVE: As Patron of the Tusk Trust and Centrepoint, Prince William launches the Cycle for Life charity bike ride in March 2008. A team of seven bikers are waiting to ride 5,000 miles through Africa to raise funds to help the locals improve their livelihoods.

RIGHT: Prince William on his first day of training in the wheelhouse of a training vessel, performing engine checks and practising manoeuvres.

LEFT: Prince William at the Britannia Royal Naval College in Dartmouth, Devon, in June 2008, where he spent three weeks undergoing basic training.

ABOVE: Prince William is taken by Royal Marines to Faslane Naval base, home of the Trident fleet of submarines on the River Clyde in Scotland in October 2007. Prince William is Commodore-in-Chief of Scotland and Submarines.

simply young men doing what young men do. If the future British monarchy is to connect with the public, isn't it a good thing that William has an understanding of his future subjects and can join them in whatever they are doing, as long as no laws are broken? Britain is an increasingly classless society and William and Harry enforce that classlessness by doing things in an ordinary way. A sense of balance is also important. Harry, in particular, has been criticized for excessive partying, but his sensitive side is the stronger part of his character and it is unfortunate that this is not as headline grabbing as his wilder side has been, as far as the tabloids are concerned. He proved himself when he was sent to Afghanistan, and much to his embarrassment was hailed as a hero, but it will only be a matter of time before he is pilloried again. William has always known how to enjoy himself, but has also always known what the boundaries are.

Diana was "The People's Princess;" the boys should be "The People's Princes" and remain the way they are. As young men they have so much time ahead of them to become conventional and formal. Despite Harry's army career and William's military training they do make time for charity work and appear to have their mother's knack of bonding with those they are trying to help.

Diana said she always watched the soaps on television so she had something to talk about with the people she met. William and Harry being "one of the lads" can have the same effect – but they have to be careful. As they face the future, both Princes know they have the love and support of their extended family to call on as they take on more royal duties and appearances. Harry's exploits on the front line and William's military involvement also provide further evidence of their love for their country and the greater good of the world.

ABOVE: Prince Harry taking part in his final exercise in Cyprus before passing out of Sandhurst, having completed his 44-week training course.

ABOVE LEFT: Prince William towards the end of his four-year course in 2004 in St. Salvator's Quad at St. Andrews University in Scotland.

ABOVE RIGHT: Prince William in his naval Sub-Lieutenant uniform. He served eight weeks in the Royal Navy from June to August 2008 on HMS *Iron Duke*.

LEFT: Prince William teaching English to Chilean schoolchildren at the Tortel School in Southern Chile when he was on his gap year with Operation Raleigh.

LEFT: The Prince of Wales and Prince William in June 2003 pose with HM The Queen at Clarence House before a dinner to mark the fiftieth anniversary of the Coronation.

ABOVE: Prince Harry, who plays in many charity polo matches, wearing a Fisi team shirt at Cirencester Park Polo Club.

RIGHT: Prince Harry playing in the final of the Queen Mother Trophy at Cirencester Park Polo Club in July 2005.

ABOVE: Prince Harry has a laugh during the Wellchild Children's Health Awards ceremony in London in 2007. The Prince does as much charity work as he can during breaks from his military career in the Blues and Royals.

LEFT: Prince Harry during his ten-week deployment to Afghanistan with his regiment.

❦ INDEX ❦

PICTURE CREDITS

The publishers would like to thank the following sources for their kind permission to reproduce the pictures in this book.

Key: t=Top, b=Bottom, I=Left, r=Right

Alpha Photo Press Agency: 65t, 68t; /Stephen Daniels: 111t, 179, 188l; /Richard Pelman: 63b; /George Phillips: 111b.

Camera Press: 32, 146t; /Kim Knott: 85; /SNOWDON: 10, 22, 26, 27, 28/9, 112; /Mark Stewart: 99b, 133, 159; /John Swannell: 6.

Corbis: /Lesley Donald/Sygma: 76, 77; /Sygma: 47t.

Getty Images: /Matt Cardy: 188l; /Adrian Dennis/AFP: 153; /Jayne Fincher: 82; /Terry Fincher/Princess Diana Archive: 24tl; /Tim Graham: 2, 15, 16b, 31, 35, 40, 42tr, 43, 44b, 45, 48, 49, 52, 54, 57, 58, 60tr, 61, 62t, 63t, 64tl, 70t, 71, 78, 83, 86, 93, 95, 102, 103l, 109, 122, 140, 150, 151, 156, 180, 181t; /Richard Heathcote: 139; / Anwar Hussein/ROTA/FilmMagic: 154; /Anwar Hussein Collection/WireImage: 13, 162; /Ian Jones/St.James's Palace: 104bl; /Keystone: 53tl; /MJ Kim: 147b; /David Levenson: 24tl, 53r; /Pool/Tim Graham: 181b; /Pool/Anwar Hussein Collection/WireImage: 165; /Pool/Princess Diana Archive: 21; /Popperfoto: 14; /John Stillwell/AFP: 144; /Mario Testino: 9; /Kirsty Wigglesworth/AFP: 117.

Mirrorpix: 61.

PA Photos: 19b, 66, 88, 106, 108, 132tr, 137, 186tl; / Chris Bacon: 98b; /Barry Batchelor: 123b; /Hugo Burnand/ Clarence House: 164; /Adam Butler: 96; /David Cheskin: 132tl; /Mark Cuthbert/UK Press: 100, 138r, 149; /Matt Dunham/AP: 146bl; /Michael Dunlea/Daily Mail: 138l, 178; /Paul Ellis: 177; /Fiona Hanson: 97; /Stephen Hird/AP: 4, 148, 160; /Ian Holding/AP: 185; /Anwar Hussein: 3, 20tr, 46t, 104t, 104br, 105, 107, 116b, 118t, 131, 136, 163, 189t; /Anthony Jones/UK Press: 155; /Martin Keene: 65b, 79, 80, 81; /Andres Leighton/AP: 146br; /Toby Melville: 110, 115, 125, 126, 128b; /Tim Ockenden: 116t; /Julian Parker/UK Press: 75t; 94, 124, 130; /Andrew Parsons: 158, 175; /Jamie Simpson: 184; /John Stillwell: 101, 103r, 141, 142, 143, 145, 161, 166, 167, 168, 169, 170, 171, 172, 173, 186tr, 189b; /UK Press: 127, 128t, 129, 186b; /James Whalting/Justin Goff/UK Press: 120; /James Whatling/UK Press: 123tr, 123tl; /Kirsty Wigglesworth: 113, 118b, 187.

Rex Features: 16tr, 20tl, 60, 67, 69b, 72, 98t, 114tl, 119, 182, 183; /David Abiaw: 114tr; /Brendan Beirne: 30, 42tl; /Eddie Boldizsar: 64b, 68b, 70b; /Mauro Carraro: 16tl, 25, 33, 35, 43b, 50t, 62b; /Paul Edwards: 50b; /Everett Collection: 19t; /David Hartley: 64tr, 69tl, 73, 89, 91; /Nils Jorgensen: 58; /Cassidy & Leigh: 1, 74, 75b; /Stephen Lock: 135; /Tim Rooke: 99tr, 152; /Sipa Press: 51, 92; /Dennis Stone: 147t; /TODAY: 46bl, 46bm, 46br, 47b, 69tl; /Julia Thorne: 12; /Richard Young: 44t.

Topfoto.co.uk: 60tl; /UPPA: 42b.

Every effort has been made to acknowledge correctly and contact the source and/or copyright holder of each picture and the publishers apologize for any unintentional errors or omissions, which will be corrected in future editions of this book.